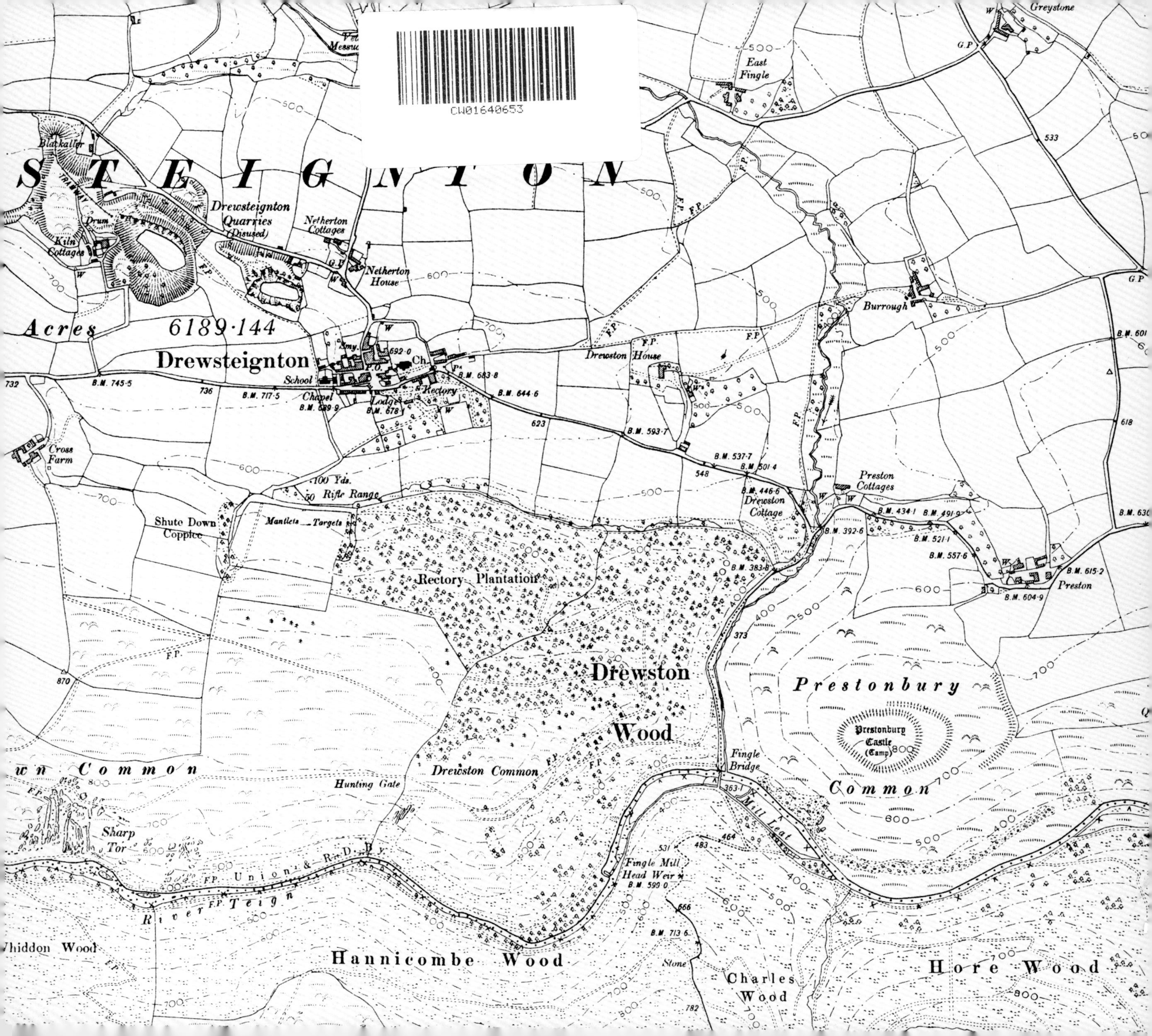

STEIGNTON
Acres 6189·144
Drewsteignton
Drewsteignton Quarries (Disused)
Blackaller
Kiln Cottages
Netherton Cottages
Netherton House
Cross Farm
Shute Down Coppice
Rifle Range
Rectory Plantation
Drewston House
Drewston Cottage
Preston Cottages
Burrough
East Fingle
Greystone
Preston
Drewston Wood
Drewston Common
Hunting Gate
Sharp Tor
River Teign
Fingle Bridge
Fingle Mill Head Weir
Mill Leat
Prestonbury Common
Prestonbury Castle (Camp)
Hannicombe Wood
Whiddon Wood
Charles Wood
Hore Wood

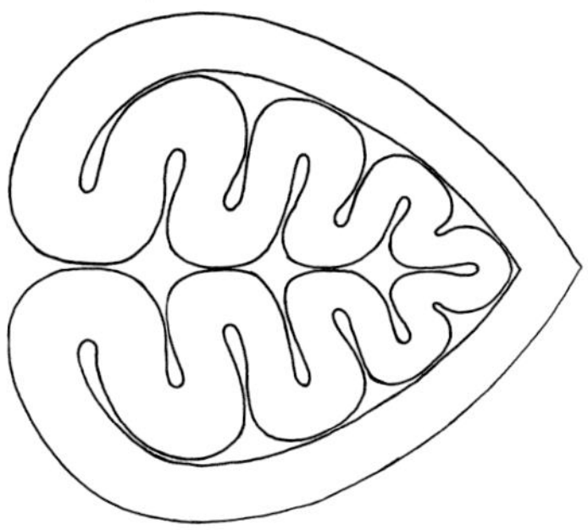

for my dear parents
Joan and Charles
Randall-Page

# GRANITE SONG

sculpture

PETER RANDALL-PAGE

photography

CHRIS CHAPMAN

essays

MARINA WARNER

JANE HAYTER-HAMES

ERIC ROBINSON

SUE CLIFFORD and ANGELA KING

A COMMON GROUND PROJECT

Published by Devon Books 1999
in association with Common Ground
with the support of
Prudential Insurance plc
Devon County Council
Dartmoor National Park Authority

# CONTENTS

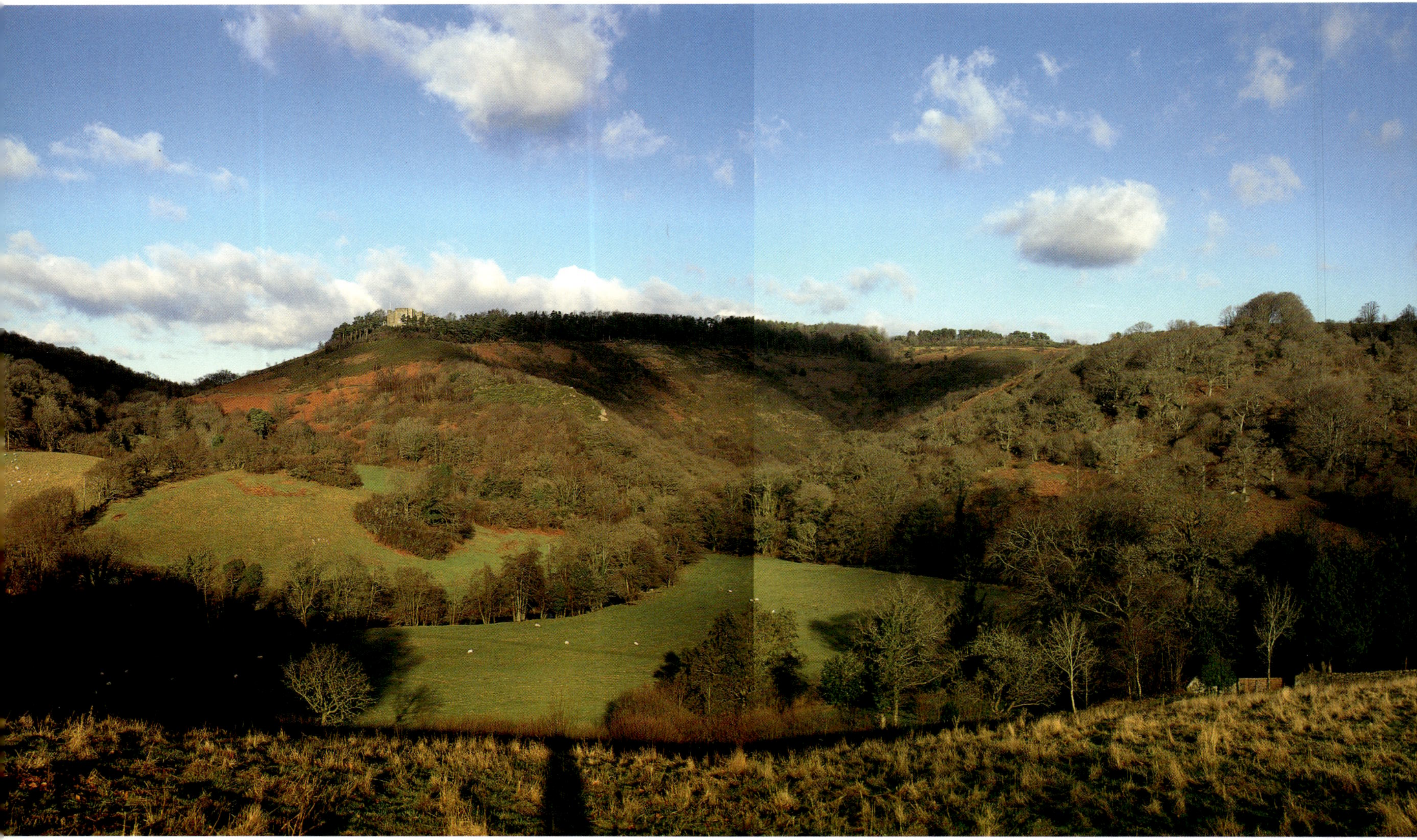

Castle Drogo, Whiddon Deer Park and the Teign Valley

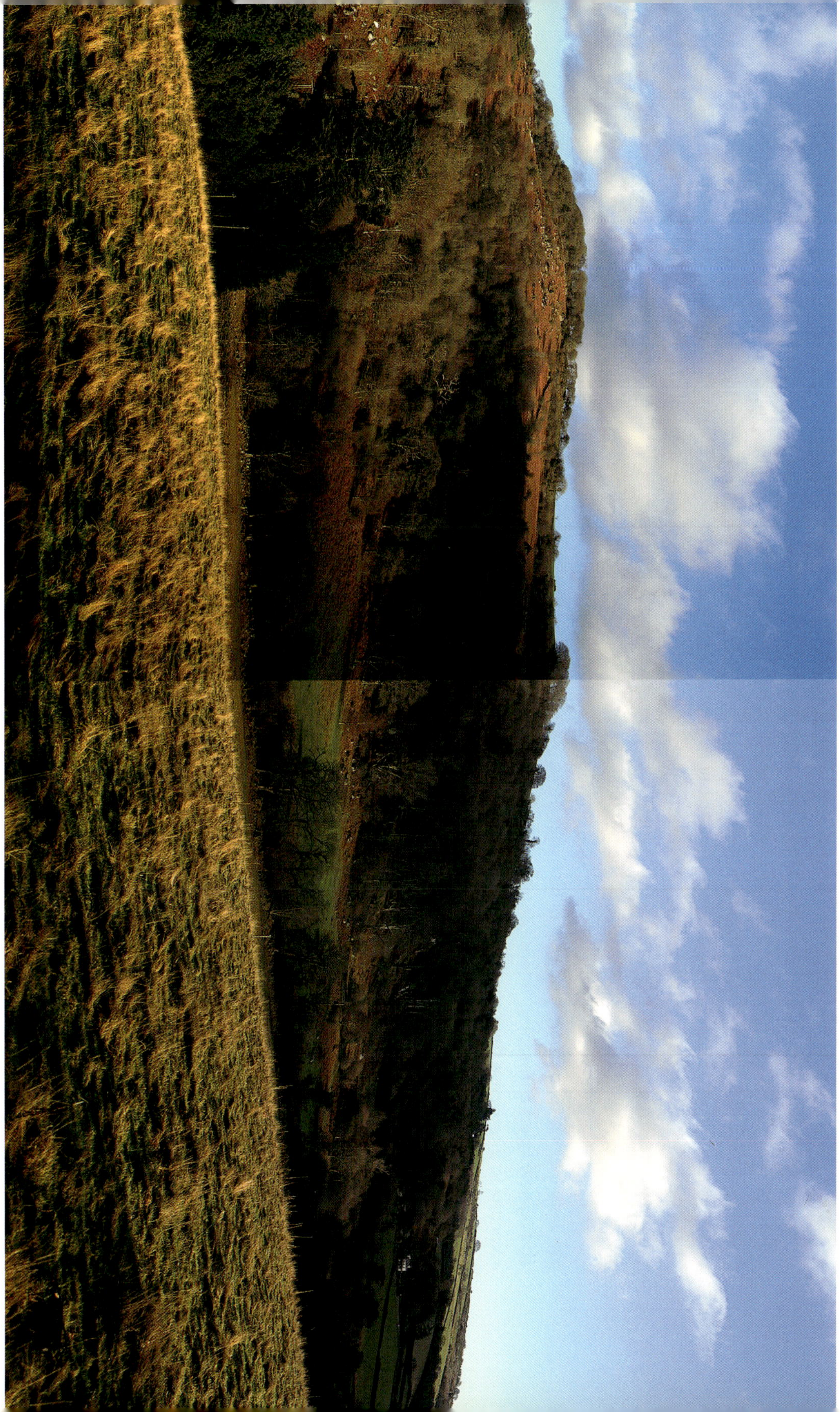

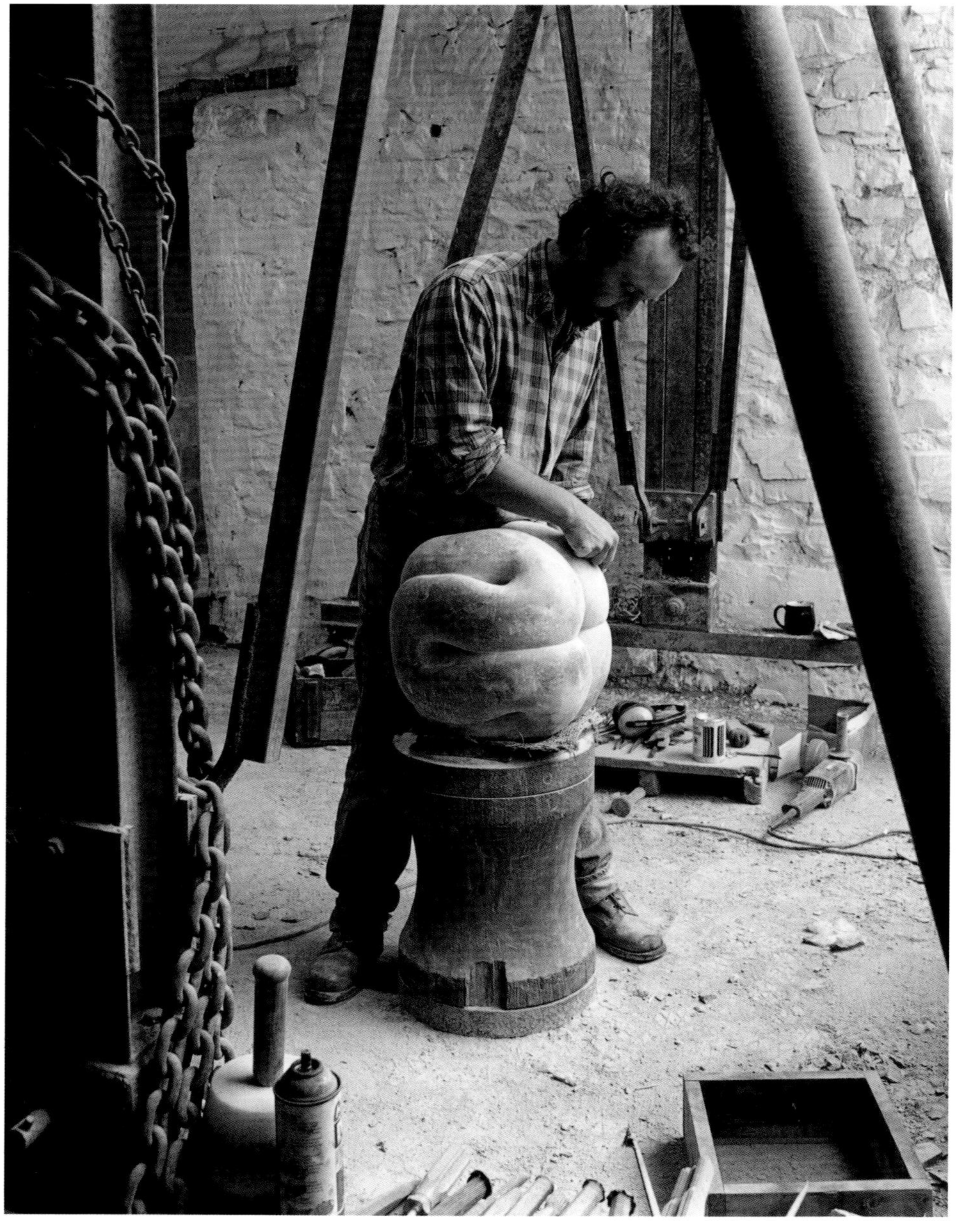

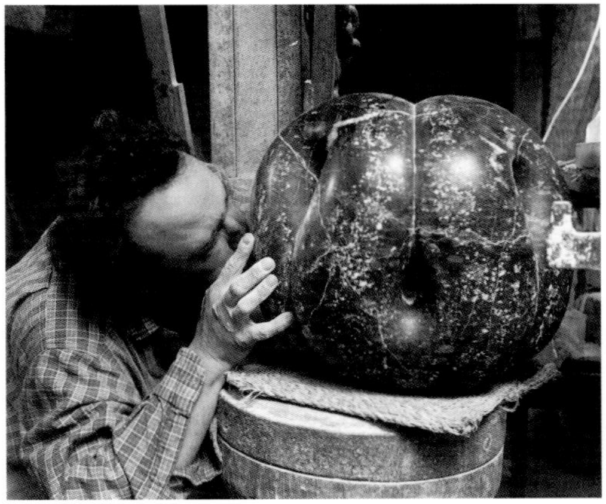

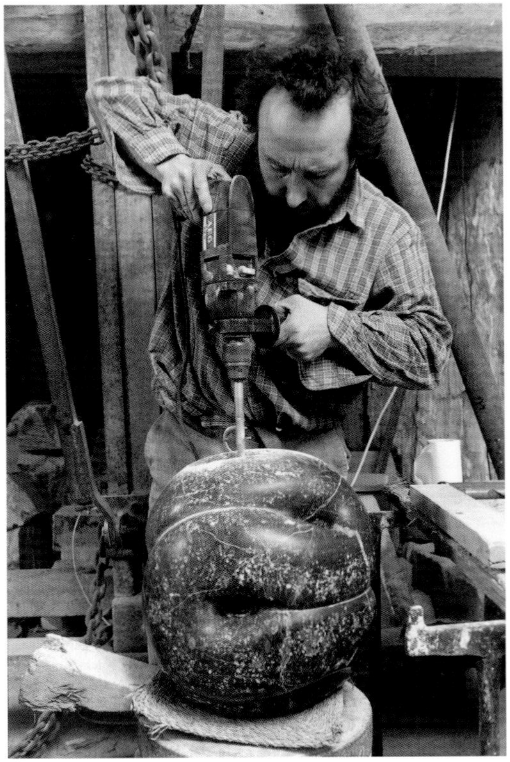

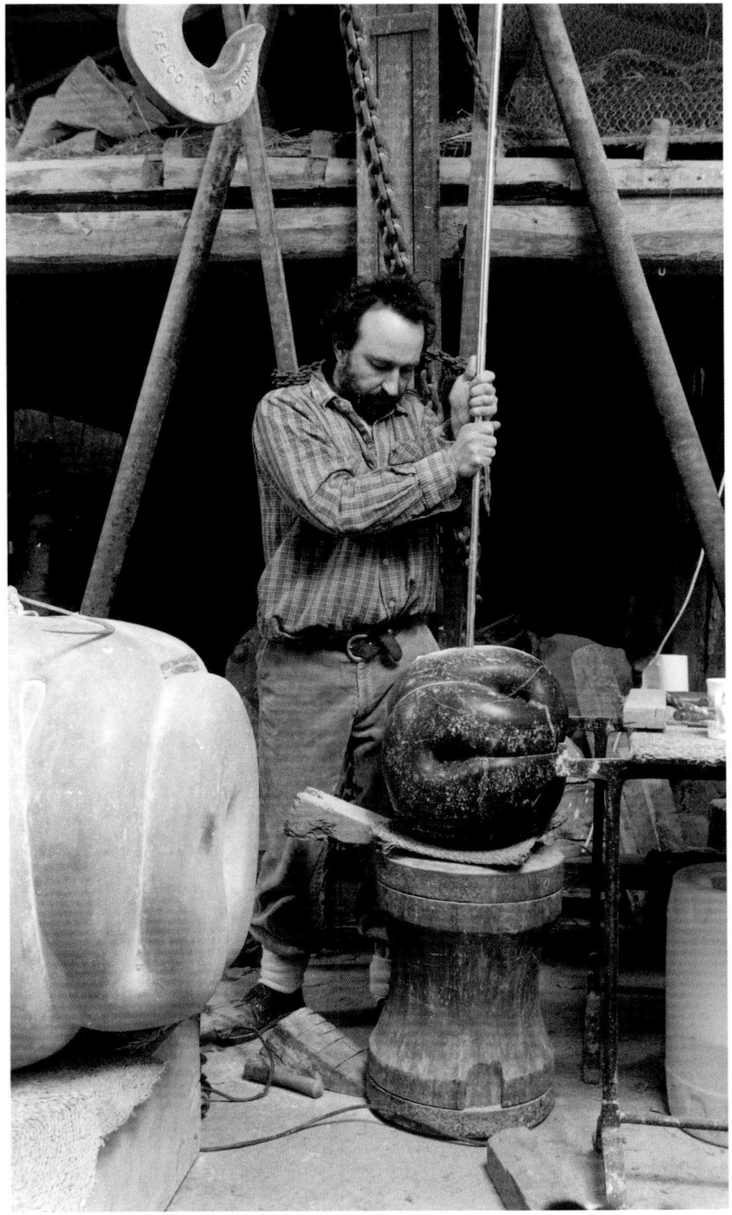

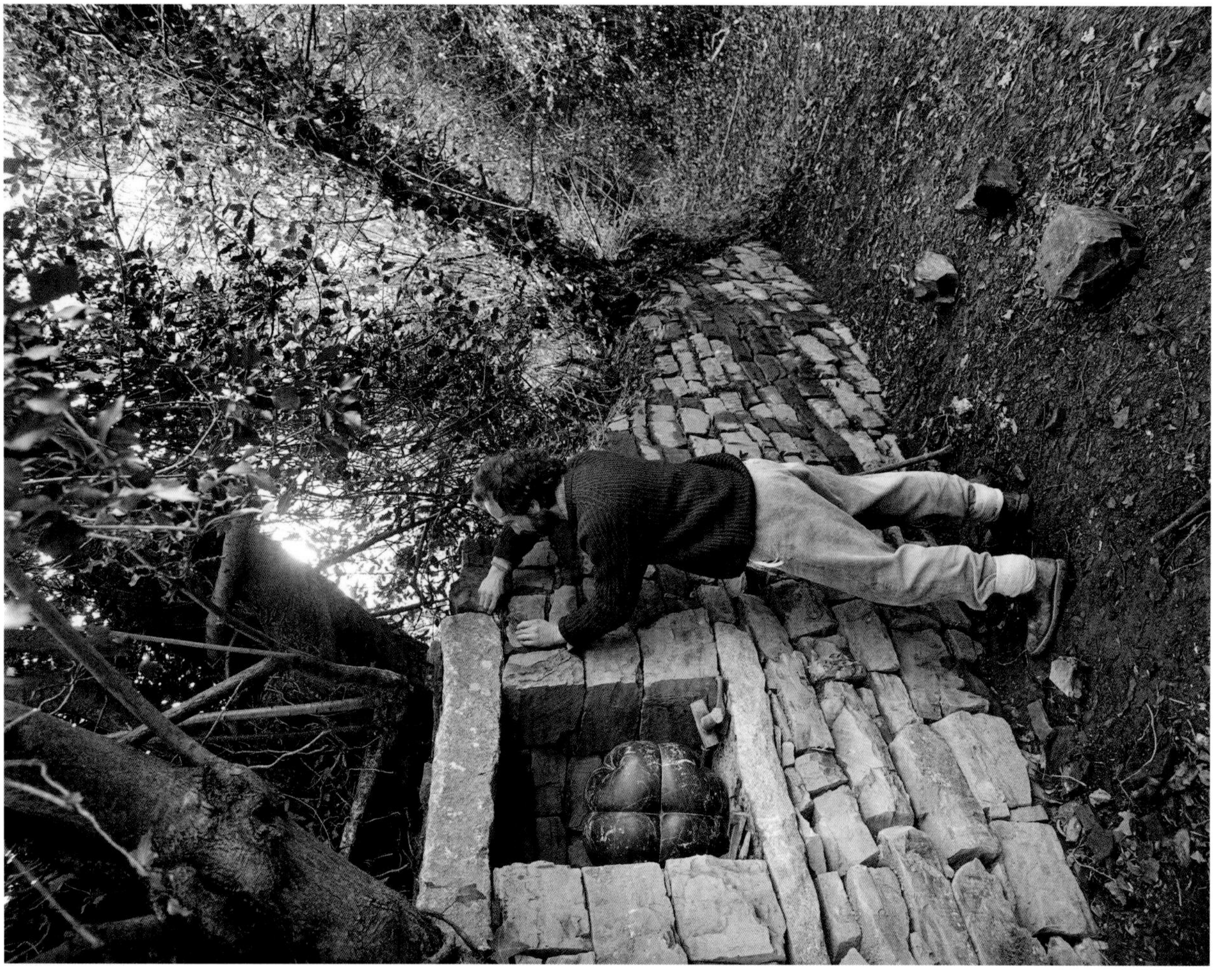

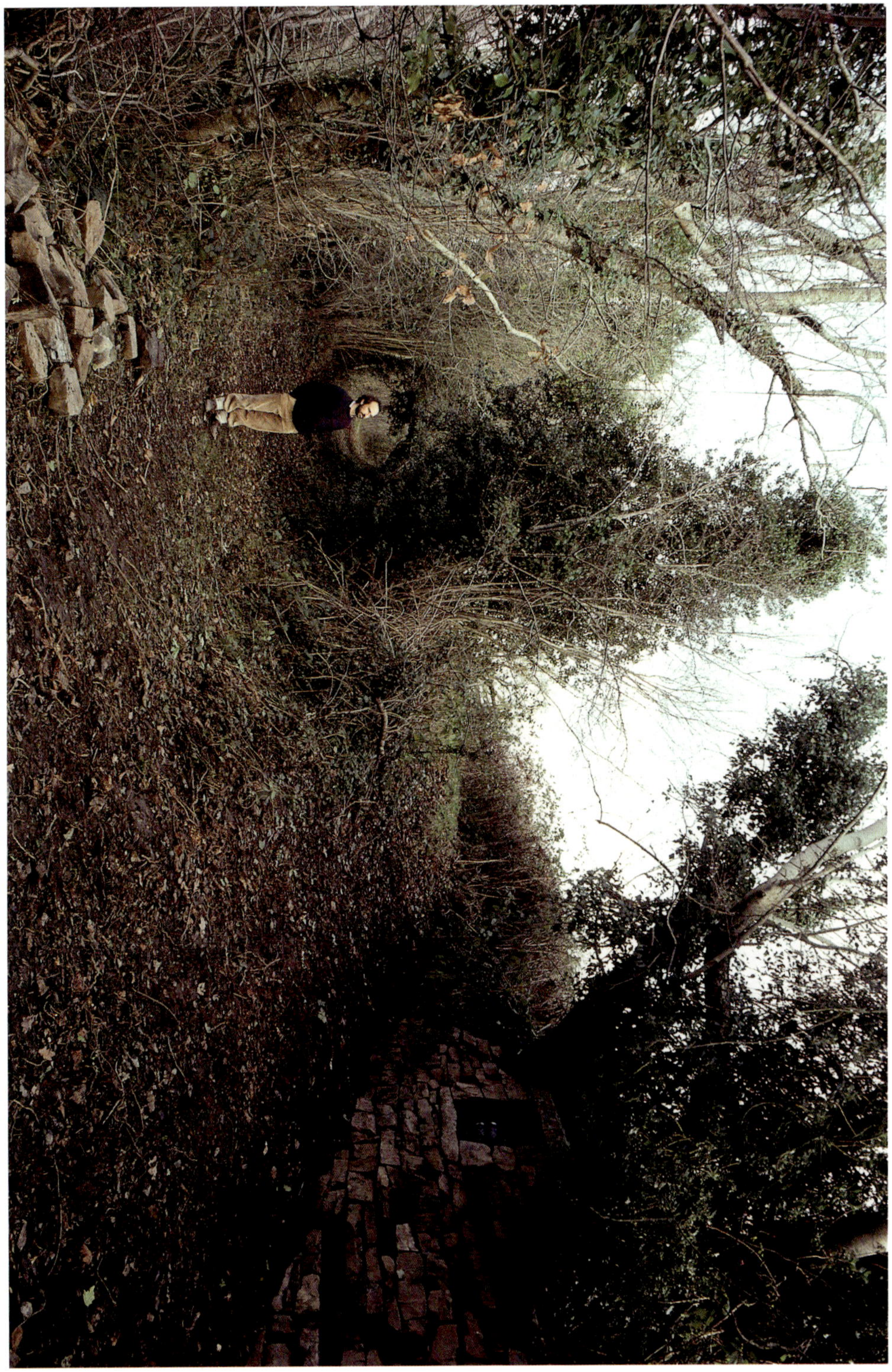

Whiddon Park, are both carved from granite. Peter Randall-Page has split the boulders to reveal the core, and then inscribed their twin inner facets with a meandering line in mirror image, as if the stone were fossils or agates hiding a secret life inside them. But granite is a rock so ancient it dates before the deposit of fossils: *'It's really primordial',* says Peter, *'pure magma'.* So the sculptor's intervention reverses the direction of geological time, and puts new life into the ancient heart of the rock, suspending its millennia of inert timelessness and returning it to the present to become a living thing again. It's revivified, becoming part of the narrative, occurring in the present time, of the visitor who breaks a path through the bracken to see it. And a new footpath has appeared on the steep hill approaching the beech avenue, where walkers have followed in one another's footsteps looking for the *Passage* that did not exist before.

The settings of the works increase the effect of vitality: the seasons transform them. Cow parsley festoons *Granite Song* in the summer, and moss is gradually filling the grooves. Peter Randall-Page has retrieved natural – alien – stone from the unstoried past, and given it a particular character, made it individual and part of the human history of that place. In doing this, he continues a tradition very significant on Dartmoor, where so many standing stones, menhirs and dolmens have previously established relationship between an unrelenting terrain and its users and settlers.[6] In the case of *Passage*, the split boulder's gargantuan scale (6 tons) makes it a direct descendant of those Cyclopean builders of the ancient British past, at Callanish, at Stonehenge.

In a fine analysis of African art, the critic T.O. Beidelman describes how the visual language of secrecy forms the crucial dynamic in the affect of sacred art. He writes that this language operates in four modes: encoding, obscurity, accumulation and containment.[7] The archetypal forms of Peter Randall-Page's work, his preferred biomorphic lexicon, relate his sculpture to ancient tribal art, as he himself readily acknowledges, and the only mode of secrecy that he has not fully adapted is accumulation – though the seriality of his drawings, especially the

[6] See Stephen H. Woods, *Dartmoor Stone* (Exeter, 1988).

[7] T.O. Beidelman, 'The Visual Language of Secrecy', in Mary H. Nooter, *Secrecy: African Art that Conceals and Reveals* (New York and Munich, 1993), pp. 49-52.

large *Fruiting Bodies,* could be said to be a form of accumulation. (Mantras, or the rosary, work through repetition: the resonant variations of those twelve huge drawings reflect liturgical use of recurring rhythms.)

All three other principles of secrecy do however animate Peter Randall-Page's works around Dartmoor: the small *Burrow Stone,* inset into a shrine-like niche low in a dry-stone wall by a gate beyond Burrow Farm, is unobtrusively placed; the two great halves of the boulder in *Passage* appear tossed aside, almost inconsequentially, by the gate; *Secret Place* – the name speaks for itself – has been ensconced by the path, a wayside shrine similar to the earliest works he made for Common Ground, on the Dorset footpath in 1985. The artist feels an evident affinity with things tucked away, lurking almost unseen, waiting to be discovered.

But the most clandestine sculpture of all is *Waterstone,* which has been stood at the foot of a leafy gully, where a steam trickles across a footpath, making a damp patch under the trees. There in the shade, near clumps of foxgloves in the dapple of light under beech, the stone oozes gently, from a navel bored through its centre; the glimmer catches the pulse of the water and winks. Peter Randall-Page abraded the granite boulder so that the trickle would bathe the stone evenly all over, as a lingam in a Hindu temple is anointed with ghee. Seeds have caught in the rough skin of the rock: tiny mosses and seedlings have sprouted; again, lifeless rock has been transmuted, to flow, to grow.

*Waterstone,* for all its inconspicuousness, nevertheless punctuates a moment in the landscape; a boggy annoyance to walkers on the path now enshrines wetness, honours the fertile compost of such ferny glades. Similarly, *Burrow Stone,* stowed safely and discreetly in the wall marks a passage in the land, where pasture, softly terraced by sheep-walks, flows down to meet tumbled woodland on the other side of the gate.

*Burrow Stone* is carved with a tight meander, raised up like the acroterion on a temple; spirals, volutes, scrolls and the continuous serpentine flow convey time in its potential mode (the snake being a well-known symbol of fertility and renewal);[8] the same meanders return

[8] See the marvellous classic of 1914: Theodor Andrea Cook, *The Curves of Life* (New York, 1979); also John Michell, *The Earth Spirit: Its Ways, Shrines and Mysteries* (London, 1989).

in *Granite Song* and *Passage.* These sinuous lines convey no intelligible meaning, as carved Ogham script or runes might, nor do they stand pictorially for a specific referent, as the fish stands for Jesus in early catacomb painting, or the mirror signifies Venus and mermaids. Yet their linearity makes them seem to resemble writing: these marks, revealed inside the stones, look as if they might be encrypting a message, and so they fulfil the function of encoding in the numinous language of secrecy. The message remains unknown – perhaps unknowable – and the sculptures become all the more affecting because they tantalise sense in this manner. Beidelman points out that secrecy in African art and ritual follows this strategy: the precise scarification of masks, for example, which transforms a face into an icon, does not translate semantically like an alphabet. Its meanings remain concealed because, at the level of ordinary sense, they do not have meaning; in that conjoining of concealment and non-sense lies much of their power, their sacred impact.

Containment dominates Peter Randall-Page's aesthetic even more than the encoding and concealing strategies of anagogic art. He is profoundly attracted to the seed inside the pod, the fossil inside the pebble, the nut inside the cone, the muscle in the coil, the form under the veil (as in the earlier sculptures *Ways to Wrap a Stone*), and has drawn and carved such emblems of futurity and fruitfulness ever since he was a boy. In his office and his studio, he keeps specimens of variously burgeoning, swelling, splitting seedcases and corms, pods and legumes from all over the world. His sculptures characteristically burrow and delve inside the rock as if it were a living thing, poking it like the sun itself into unfolding, uncurling – into efflorescence, lighting up the cockles in its dormant heart. But in the sculptures for Devon, he hasn't chosen to carve the fruit or the seed, at either end of the cycle of growth. Rather, he's taken the clenched time in between, when ripeness is all potential: to express this, he plays with the idea of containment, and reaches for imagery to suggest what might be hidden inside. The fossils of *Granite Song* and *Passage* open to show their mysteriously engraved heart: *'There's an exhilaration about walking through the middle of what was a solid thing'*, he says. *'Everything we make is boxes – houses, cars, containers – but there's something very different about a stone that's solid through and through. It's just stuff – matter'*. *Secret Place* keeps its secrets tightly clasped; *Waterstone* enigmatically makes a gift of water from its pierced core. As Peter says, *'It was literally like getting blood out of stone'*.

Thinking on his art as a whole, he comments, *'The whole enterprise is not to feel like a disembodied consciousness wandering through the world. I know that we are all deeply connected. There's a difference between intellectual knowledge and knowledge of a different kind, like when you sit down and play an instrument – a physical knowledge, connecting us as part of everything, with the trees and with Douglas [his dog] and with stories and the past and the future. The illusion of being separate and being lonely isn't the real state of affairs'.*

Institutional churches with their eye trained on the hereafter have obscured the less grandiloquent, fundamentally secular idea behind the word *'religio'*, which comes from the Latin, and means to bind together again, experience undergone and renewed in common to create mutuality and reciprocity, to beat the bounds of a shared history, to mark, as Peter Randall-Page's sculptures do, the ways we walk, sometimes alone, sometimes not, as we trace memories into the mind from things seen, as we draw desire paths.

# GRANITE SONG 1991

Dartmoor granite
70 x 84 x 40cm, 70 x 84 x 40cm

Located on a small island in the middle of the River Teign on private land,
but visible from the Two Moors Way footpath between Drewsteignton and Chagford.
OS map ref. SX710890

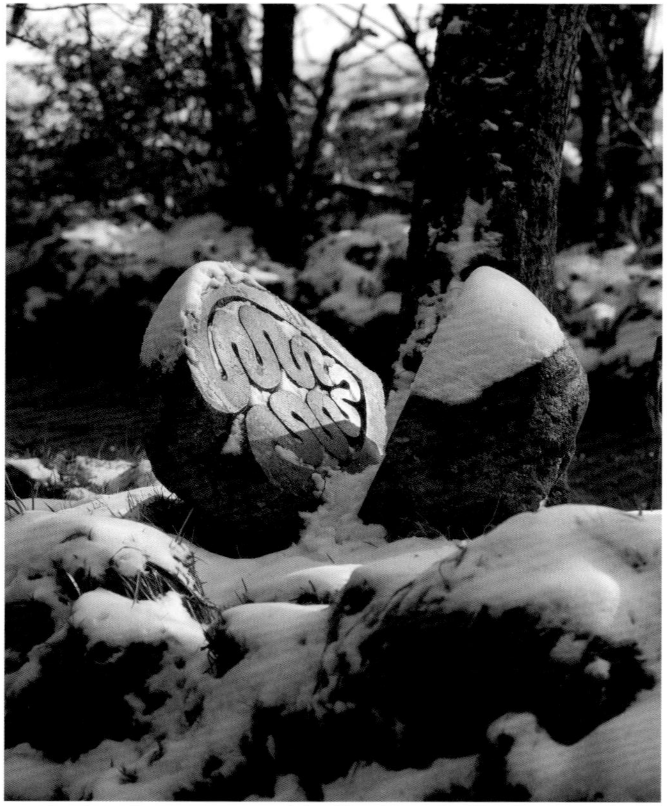

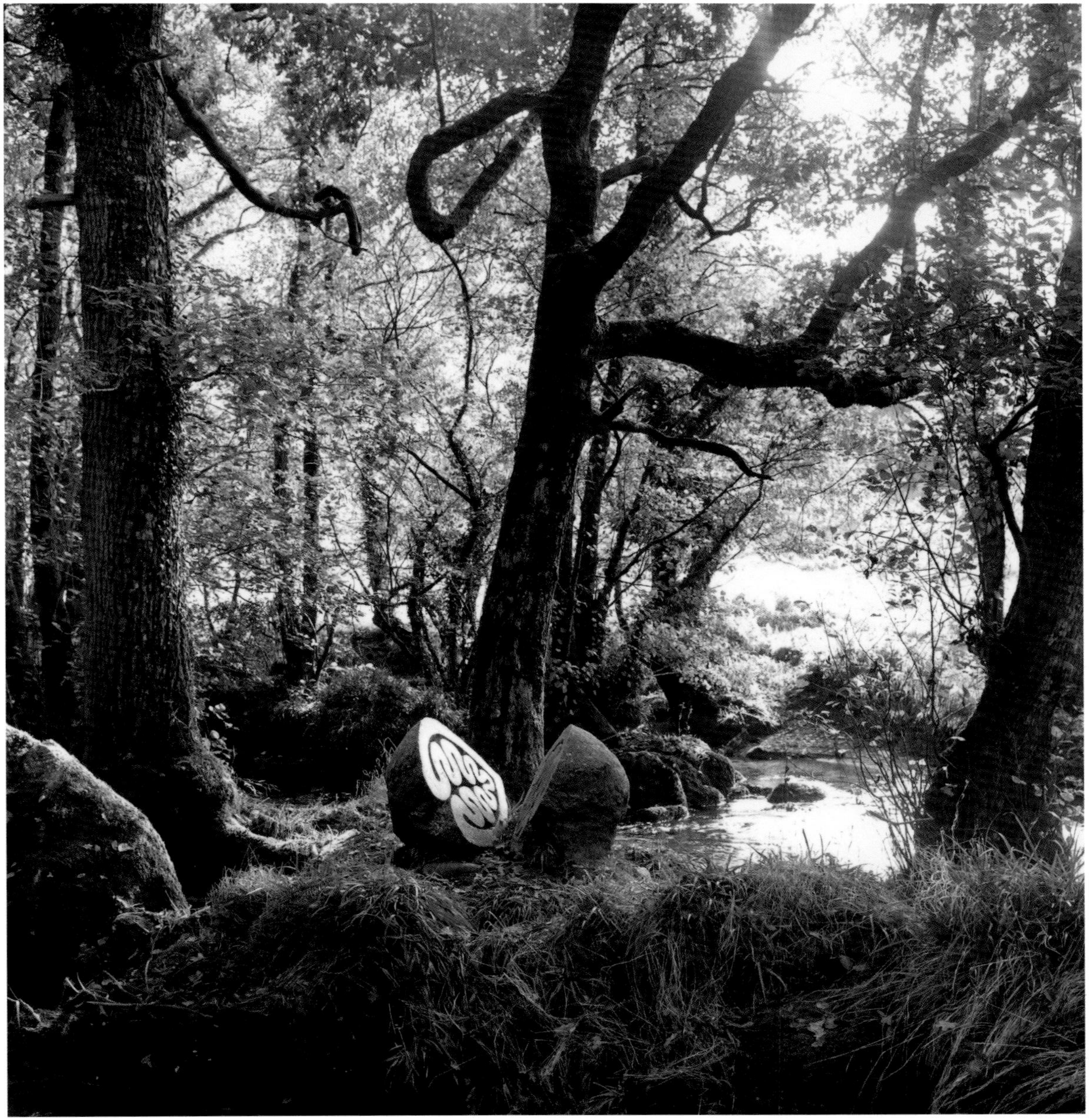

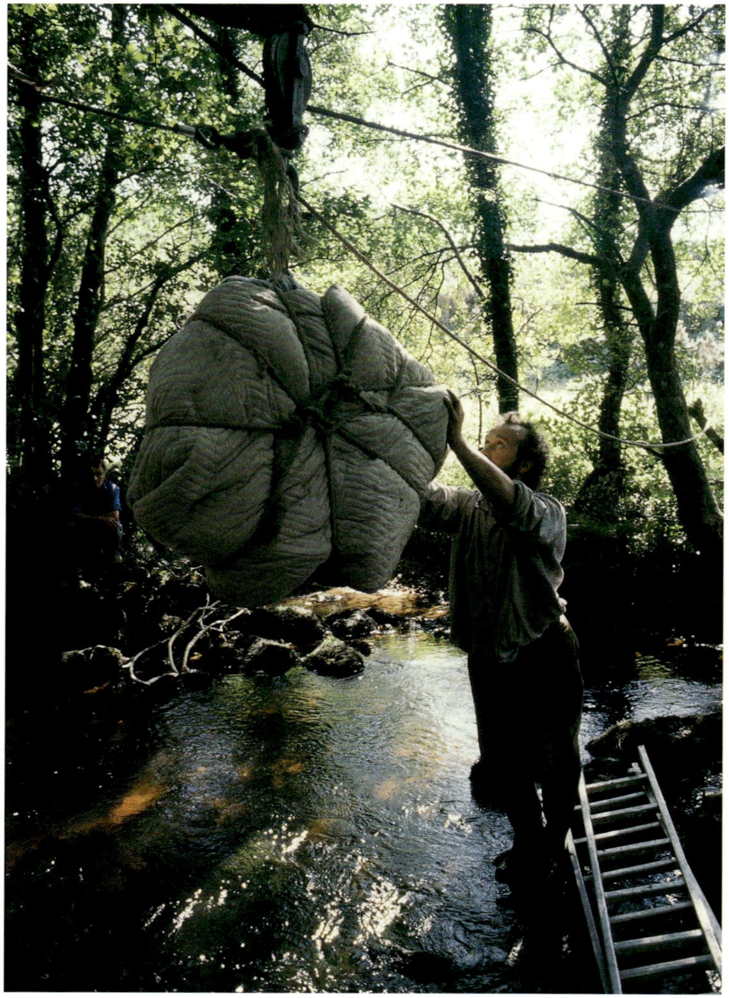

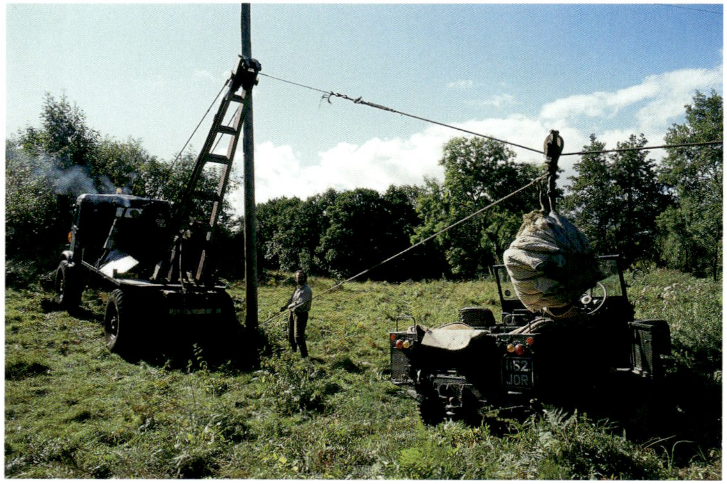

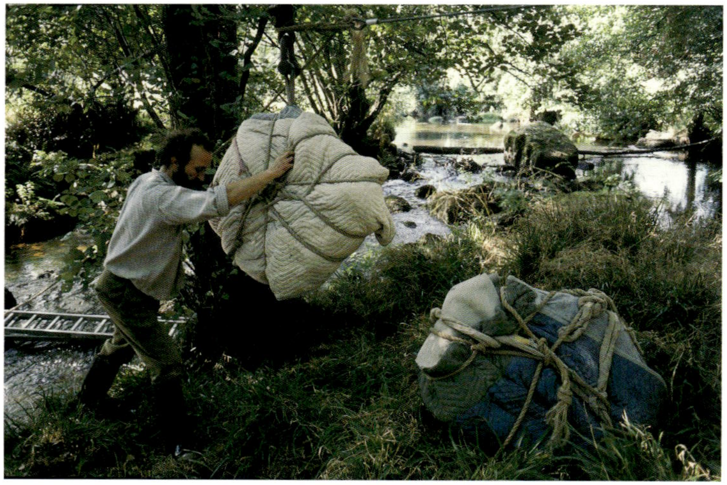

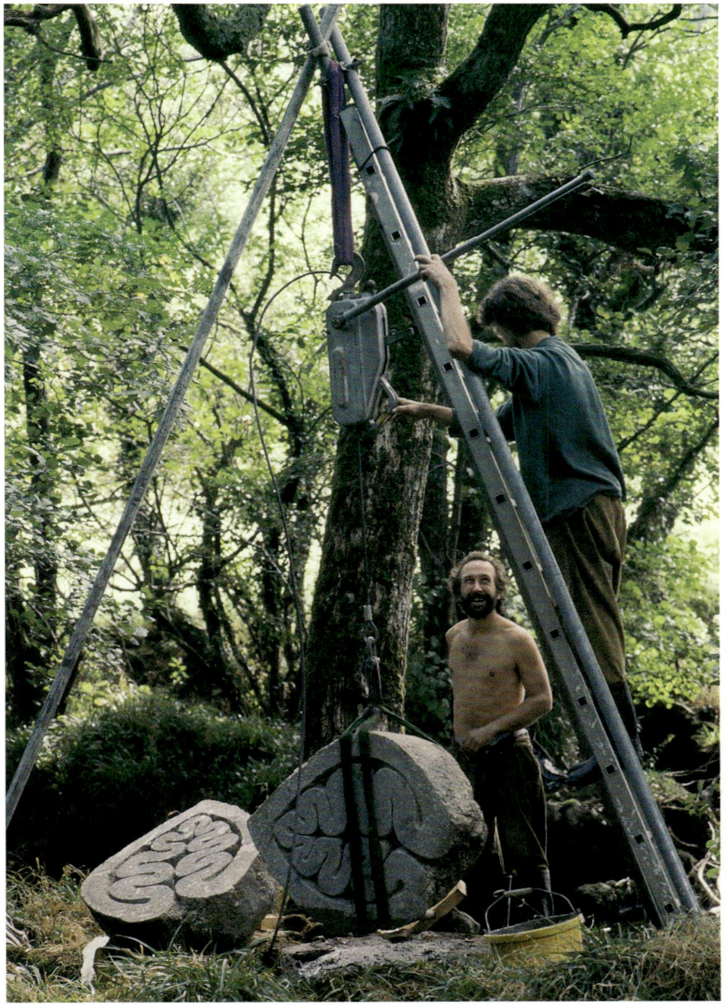

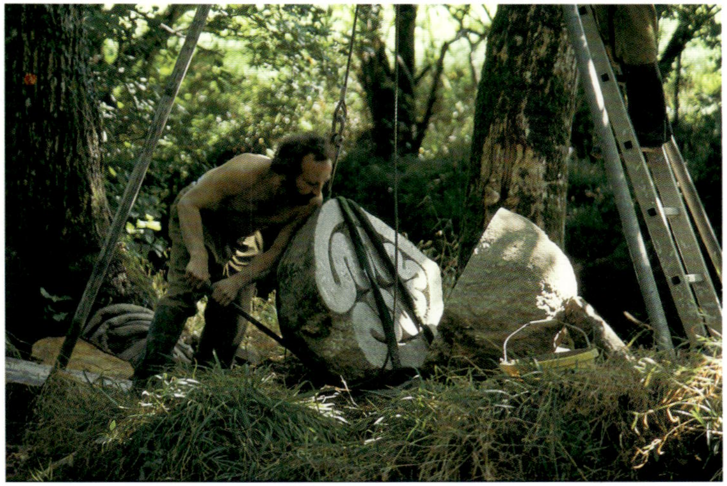

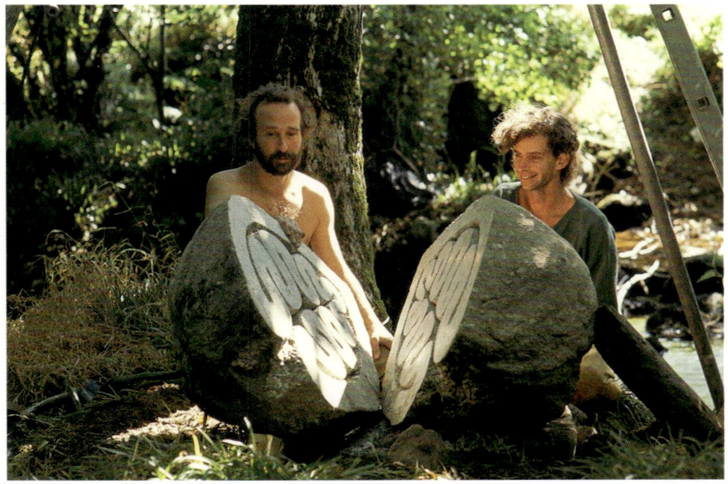

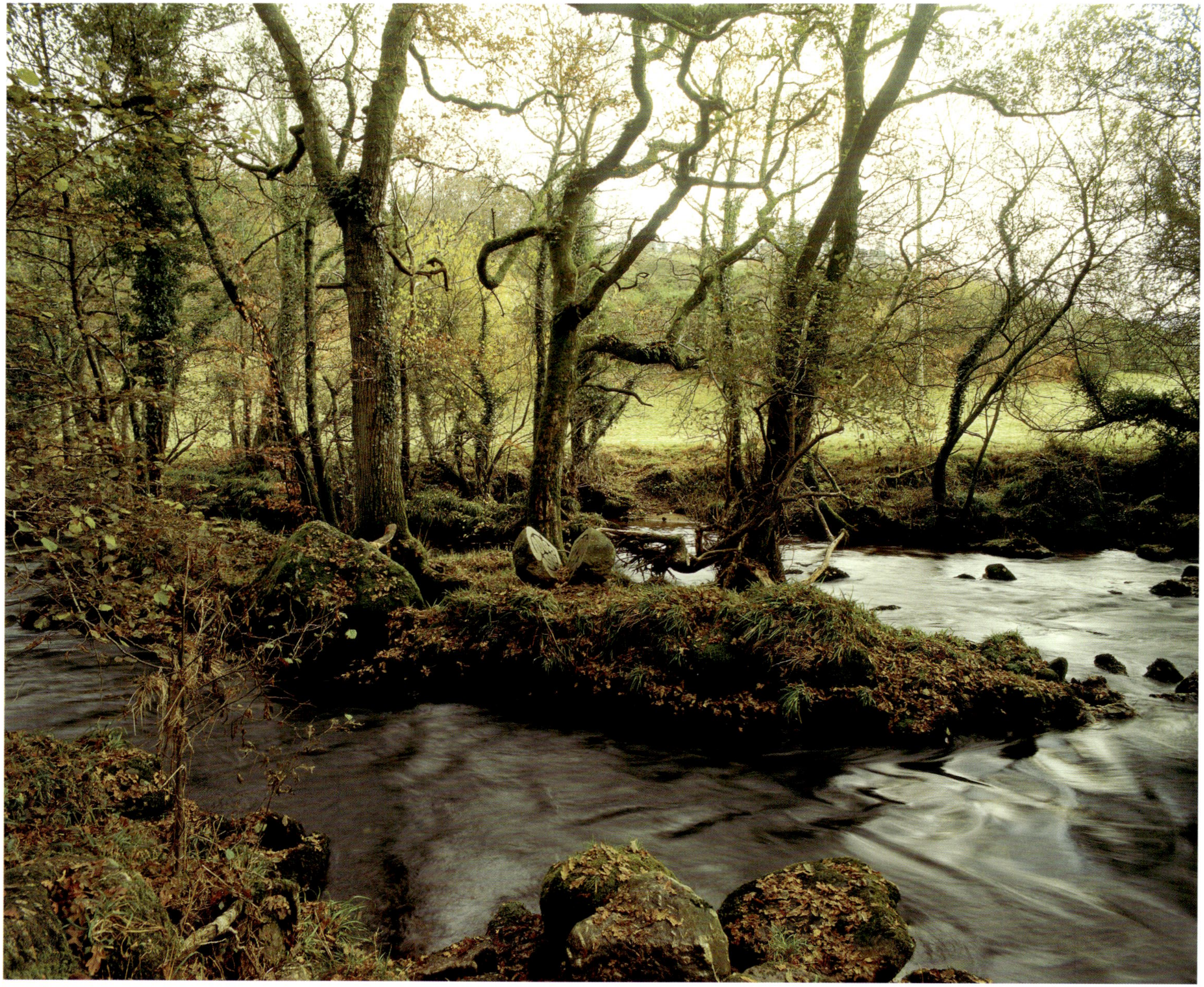

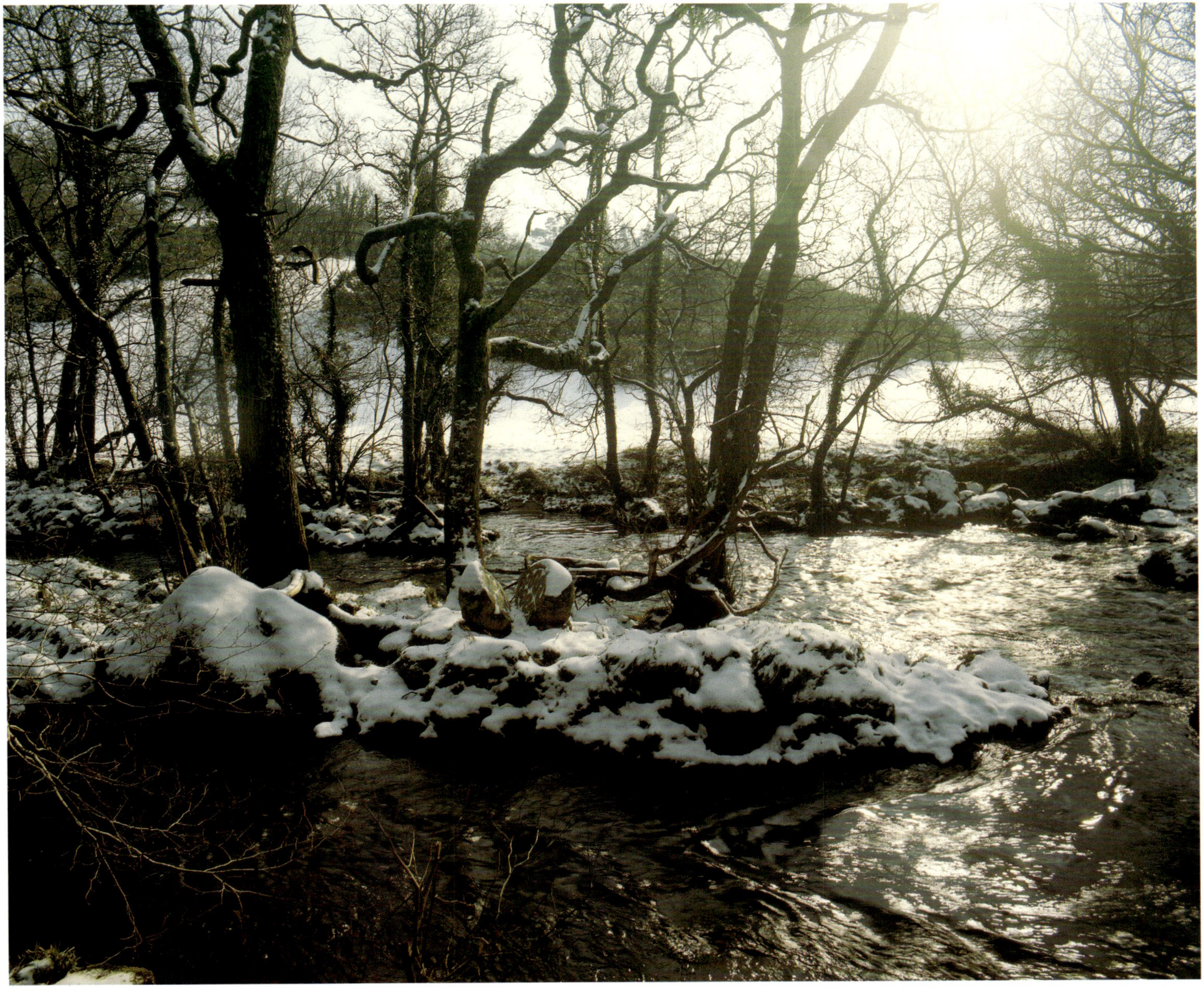

capacity at a time when the climate was changing. The acid peat, combined with the browsing animals which nibbled the saplings, decimated the sparse tree cover.
The Dartmoor landscape was being formed.

With standing stones and rows, with burial mounds and stone circles, living in clusters of round huts of stone and thatch, the peoples of Dartmoor fused together into a highly sophisticated culture. The resources of the moor for grain growing and for grazing were stretched. But now Dartmoor dwellers were not only engaged in subsistence agriculture, they were smelting and exporting tin.

It was sea-faring strangers who bought the precious metal. Used as an alloy in bronze, it was found in ore on the surface of the granite upland, and later became the source of mediaeval Devon's wealth and power.

Dartmoor has lead, zinc, copper, silver and gold in very small quantities. But the surface metal, and the one which occurred in greatest quantity, was tin.

Drewsteignton stands just north of the Teign Gorge. Where hill forts of this period (Cranbrook, Prestonbury and Wooston) overlook the deep ravine. From here, Celts with iron swords commanded both the river and the old track-way to the Moor. In Ireland and Brittany, their culture flowered and endured to leave the classic Celtic designs of interwoven curves and spirals, seen on early churches in western Britain.

Romans built straight roads, but Devon is curved and folded. In exasperation, they by-passed Dartmoor and its precious metals and took their road in a straight line on towards Cornwall. A flourishing Roman city grew up at Exeter and into it came the first whisperings of Christianity.

The word had already spread up the valleys and among the hill peoples. Around the coast, early Christian mystics and Celtic saints had settled. From them, the new religion spread through the tribal peoples of the south-west. On the wave of the coming of Christianity and the leaving of the Romans, rose our last mythical King.

Arthur, King of the Britons, lived on the watershed between Celtic Paganism and Christianity, between Imperial Rome and the Dark Ages. He lived at the end of the Gaelic oral tradition which, in England, survived solely in his legend. An historical leader, who also gathered older tales around his story, so that it comes to us part history, part myth. He rode through the south-west gathering the tribes to fight the new invaders, the Saxons. After his death, the Saxons created their fiefdoms which were consolidated into the kingdom of England.

Slowly the Saxons infiltrated the hill country of the west. Gradually they made farmsteads in the steep valleys sloping down from the high moor. By slash and burn they cleared the forest. They pushed the granite boulders together to form walls, tipped earth on top to get height and trees grew up to form the dense hedges that line the Devon lanes. The nature of the bedrock had forced the agricultural decision and a distinctive landscape resulted: granite, metal and water have always determined the patterns of settlement on Dartmoor.

By the 12th century, tin was once more being worked in large quantities and the churches owed their size to the wealth coming from tin. On the moorland edge, accessible to packhorse, Chagford administered its own stannary district and became a 'coinage' town where the tin was weighed, assayed, taxed and sold. On market days merchants came from all over the country and from abroad, travelling the ancient track-way from Exeter to buy smelted tin.

On mediaeval Dartmoor, two industries competed: tin and wool. The tinners were free men, owing their feudal dues directly to the King and in the Middle Ages, the wealth of the Stannaries endeared the tinners to the Crown. Their rights over-rode those of the farmers. By the 1640s, woollen merchants were powerful, their interests triggered the Civil War. On Dartmoor loyalties were split. The Whyddon family of Chagford, for example, was involved in both the tin and woollen industries and were divided – some supporting the king and others parliament.

The Whyddons, long a local family, owed their rise to Sir John Whyddon, who died in 1575. A Judge of the King's Bench in the reigns of Queen Mary and Queen Elizabeth I, he was

## WATERSTONE 1992

Granite boulder and water
115 x 84 x 80cm

Located on the side of a public footpath crossed by a small stream through Rectory Wood (National Trust) between the Two Moors Way and Hunters' Path, south of Drewsteignton.
OS map ref. SX736906

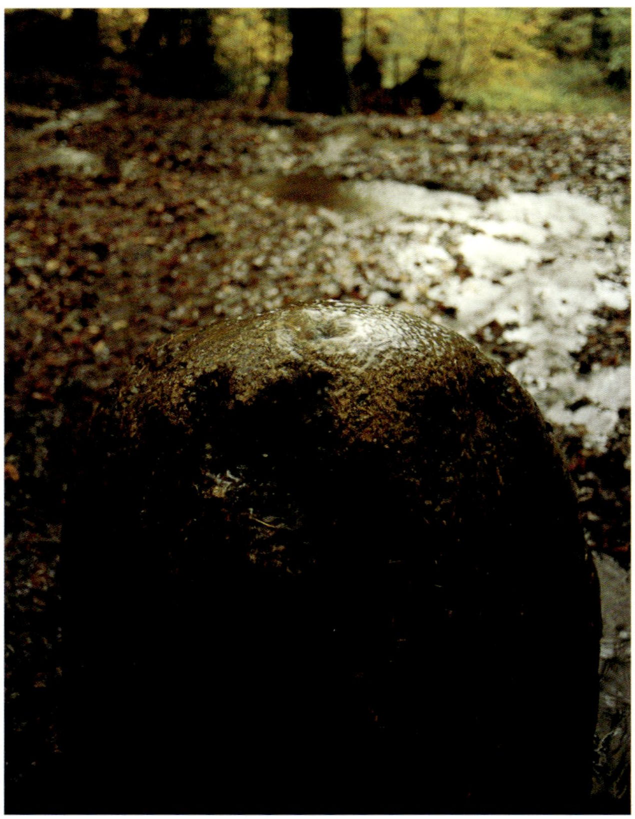

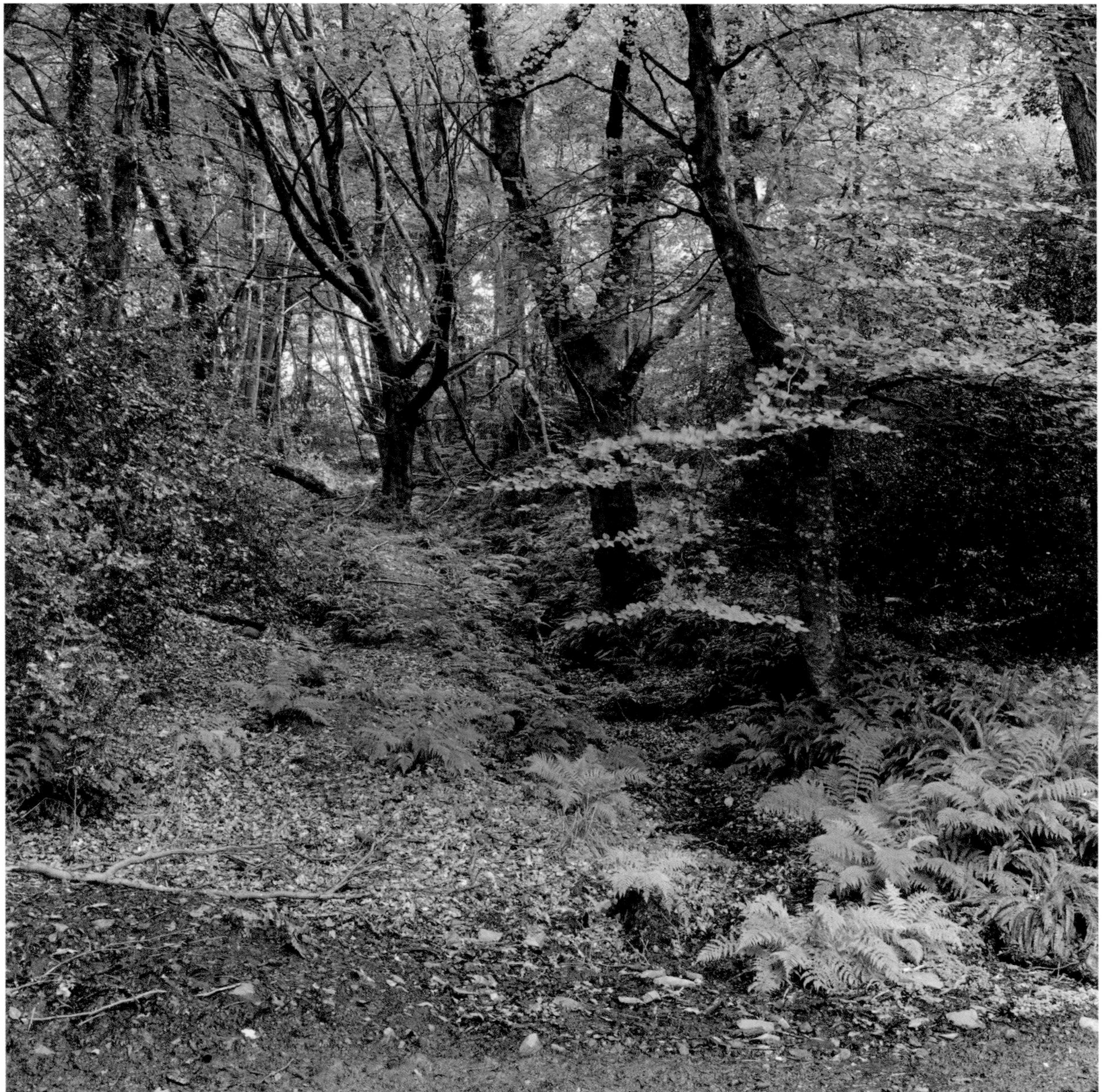

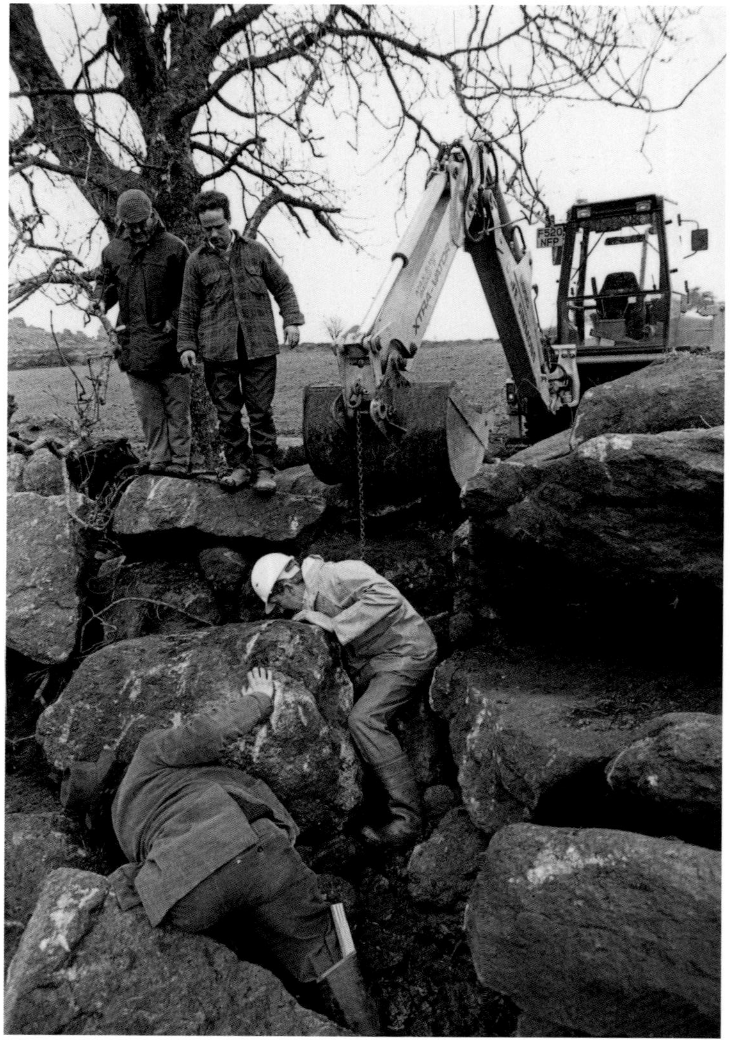
F520
NFP
XTRA-VATOR

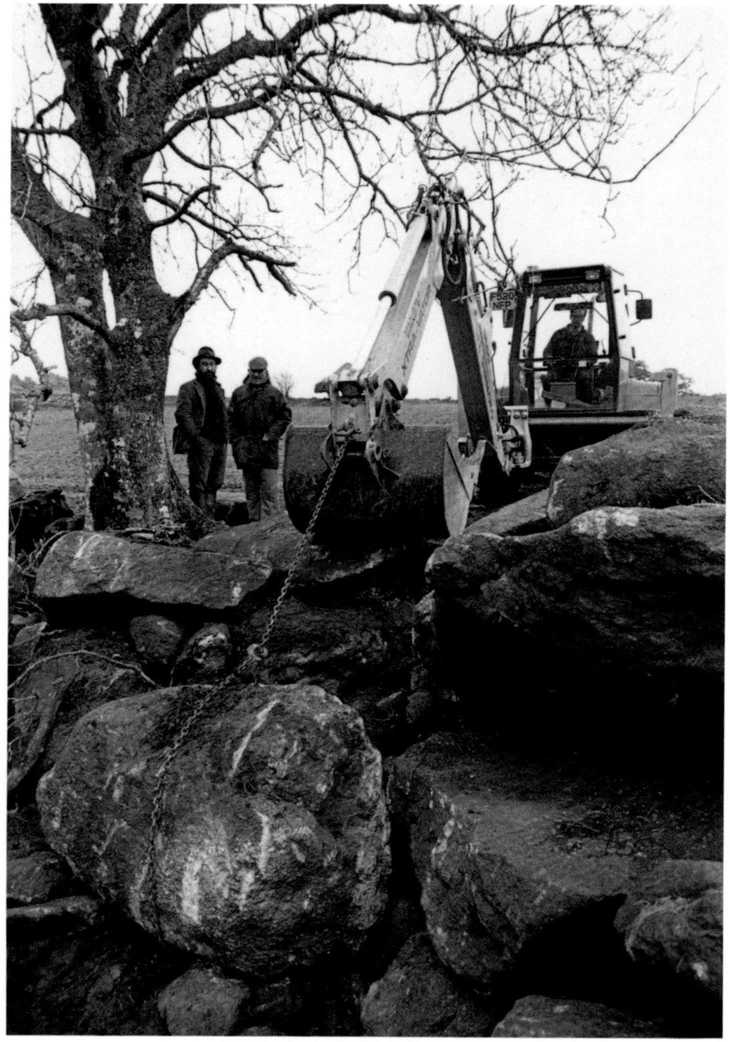
F520
NFP

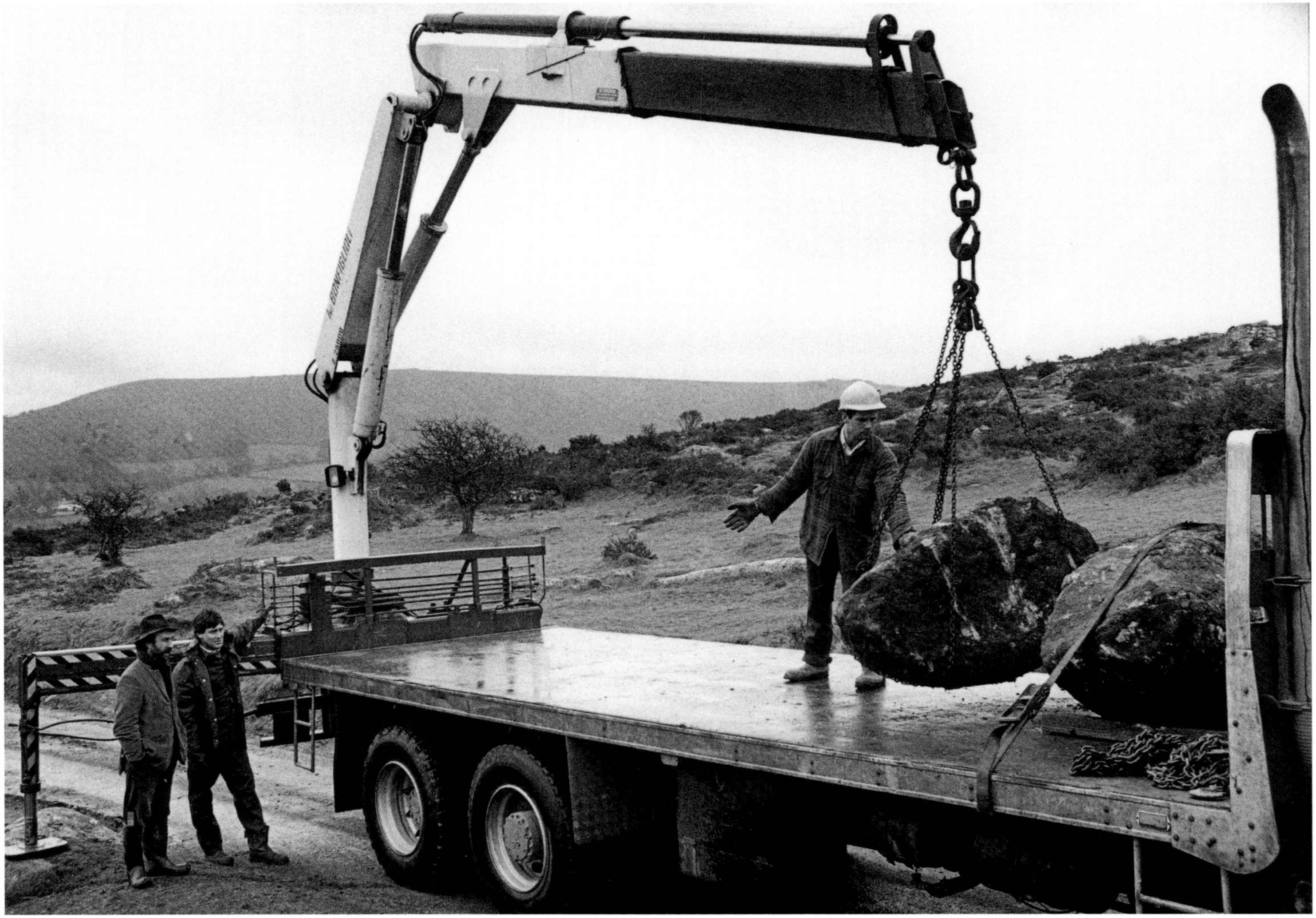

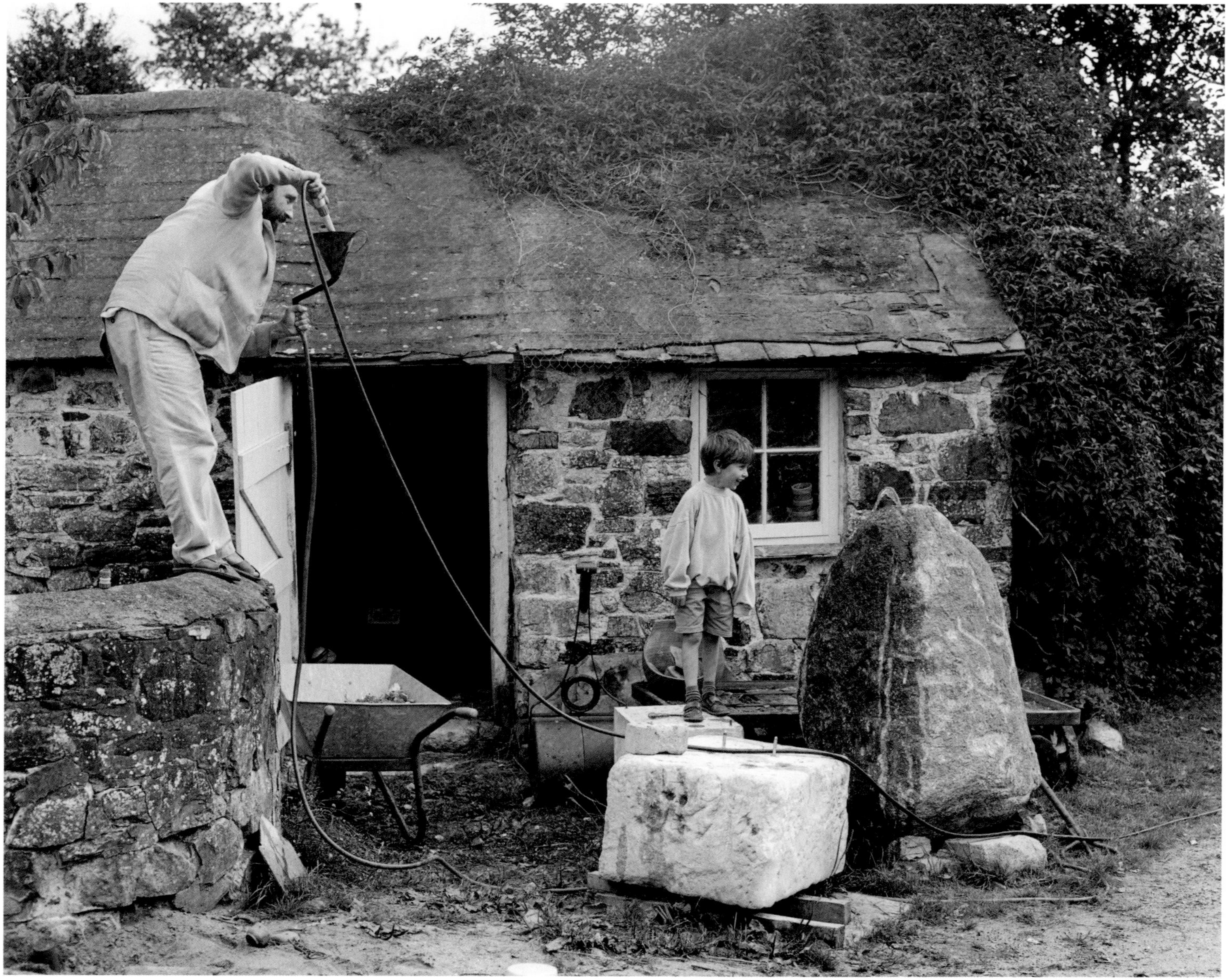

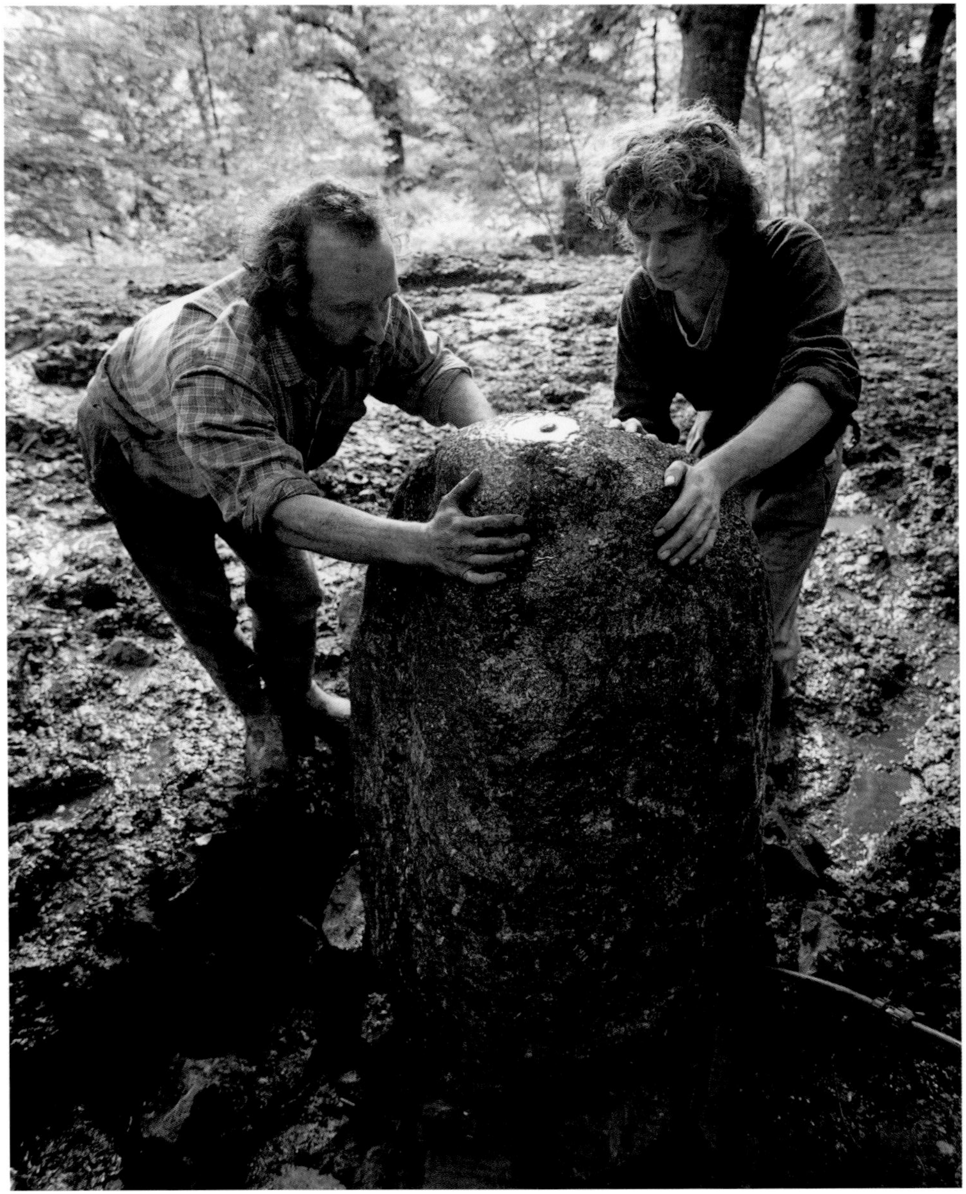

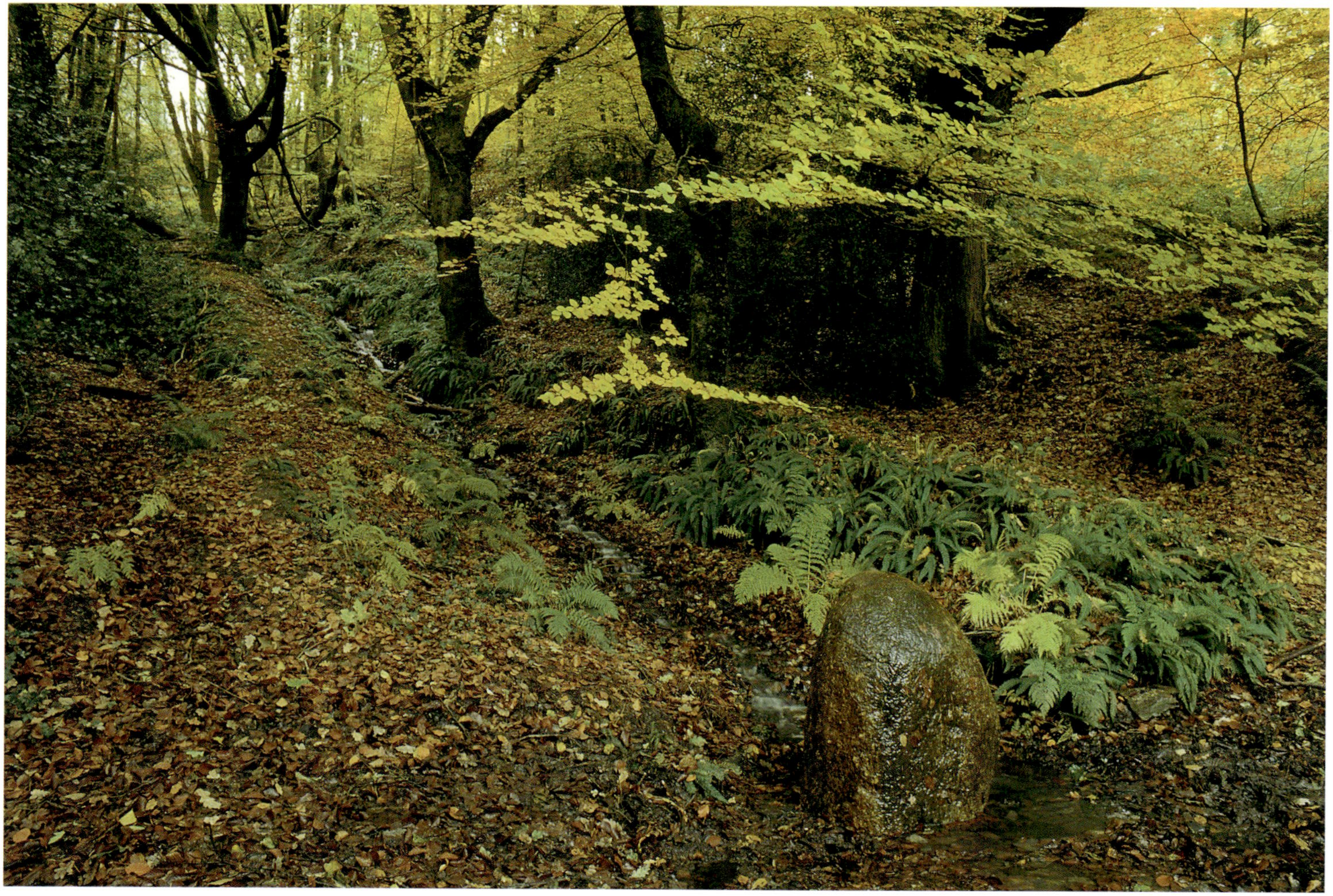

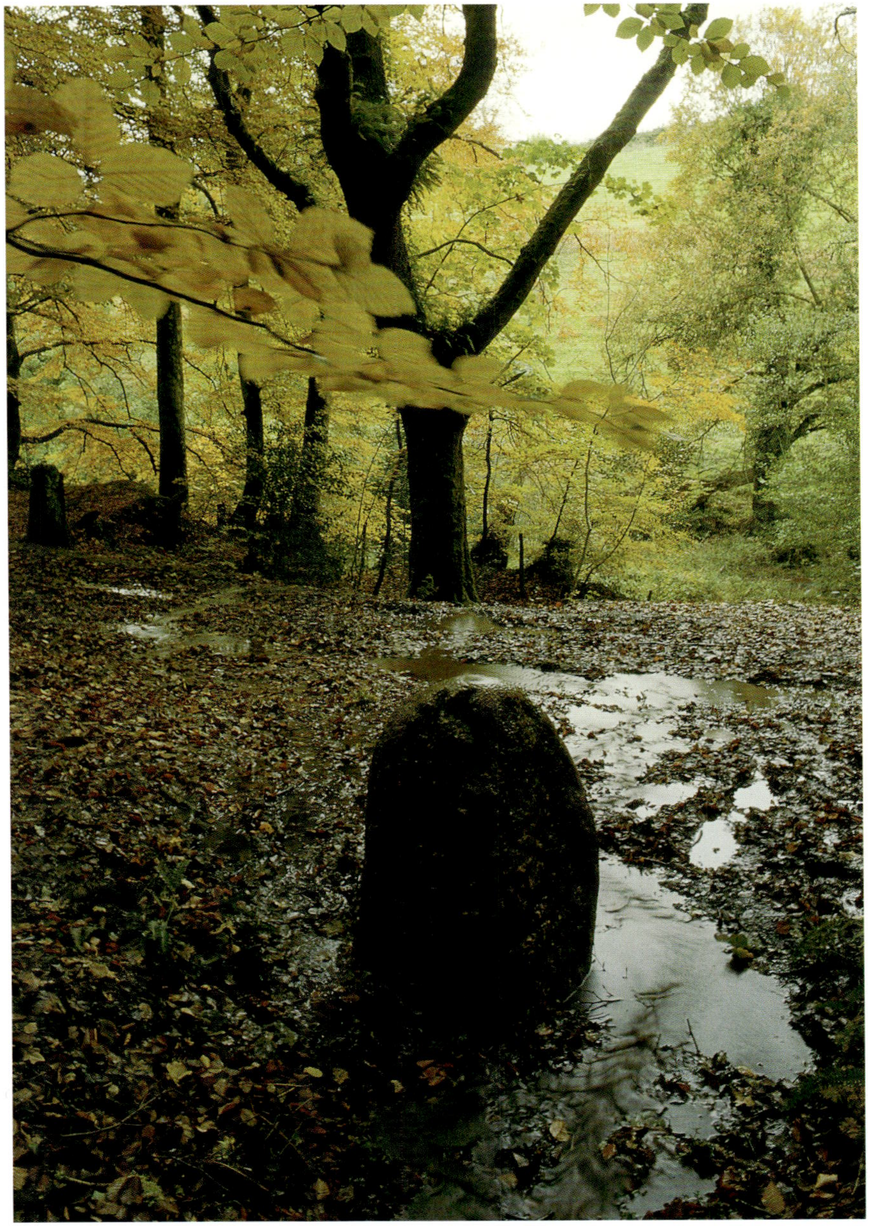

# GRANITE

Eric Robinson

By a lucky chance, Peter Randall-Page has accepted as one of his most important materials the rock type which, above all others, has magical qualities for the geologist. Granite has always posed more questions than any other rock, but at the same time, has triggered speculations which verge upon the mystical. There are many characteristics in granite which we can measure and interpret by direct observation and draw meaningful conclusions. These conclusions are as close as geologists can get to being scientific and logical, but others will always remain which lie beyond experiment or observation – the residual and necessary mystery. The extra-special attraction of Geology as a Science must be the scope it gives to the imagination. If we start with the obvious features of the stone – best seen when washed by rain or in the river bed or best, of all, on the polished surfaces of a gravestone in the churchyard – it must be the texture resulting from the interlocking shapes of the rock-forming minerals that sparks our imagination – a jig-saw puzzle of quartz, feldspar, and flakes of mica if we want to be technical. With the logic of children, these minerals are the visible 'grains' of the grain stone, granite.

Closer study of those grains take us back some two hundred years to re-enact one of the classic debates in the history of Geology, a debate which centred upon the Mining Academy in Freiberg in Saxony and the meeting places of the Royal Society of Edinburgh. To some natural scientists, granite was the crystalline end-product of a universal ocean, rich in minerals in solution which, in due course, separated out and grew in the fashion of copper sulphate crystals that can be 'grown' in the laboratory. Those who held this watery view of the origin of granite have become known to us as the Neptunists in the course of time. There was, however, a contrary view which saw crystalline granite as the result of the cooling of a rock melt comparable with the molten lava which flowed from the active volcanoes, volcanoes familiar to those who had made The Grand Tour, visiting Naples or Sicily. To them granite was molten rock which had cooled, congealed and crystallised deeper in the crust of the earth, beneath the roots of the active vents such as Vesuvius or Etna. Appropriately, their school of thought took the name of the God of the Underworld and they became know as the Plutonists. Whichever view was favoured, both shared one observational criterion which remains valid today: whether minerals formed from hot melt or supersaturated brine, their size and perfect form speak of slow and constant growth, in contrast to other irregular and untypical shapes with stunted growth which speak of haste and sudden consolidation. Sometimes, one mineral may show near-perfect crystal form and grow to an exceptional size, in comparison to other minerals. Logic would say that this mineral was the first to form, stealing a march on its associates; geological semantics would say that this rock was Porphyry and its texture porphyritic.

As it happens, it was astute observation of such early growth minerals which went to solving the Neptunist-Plutonist controversy as far back as 1787 when Dr. James Hutton, a prominent member of the Edinburgh school, was walking the banks of a Highland stream. To the surprise of his colleagues, he plunged into the water to study, at close quarters, thin veins of pink granite penetrating the darker slaty rocks of the Highlands. Discerning that crystals of a pink mineral found in the granite could also be seen within the black slaty rocks, he rightly deduced that granite had come later in a time sequence, invading the pre-existing slaty rock. What was more, the contacts between the two rocks was of a kind which could be compared to the burning of one by the other. The molten origins of granite were demonstrated.

These same observations can be made in the streams draining from Dartmoor, the granites altering the local slaty rocks (the killas of local terminology in the South West), or the less frequent limestones of the Teign Valley near Drewsteignton, in ways which could be contrived in a furnace or a seasonal bonfire which reddens stones that come within the 'hearth'. Contacts between granite and what we would call 'country rock' are a fascination for geologists coming new to the area. To them, there is the fulfilling experience of repeating the observations of Dr. Hutton, assembling the facts as they can be determined and, hopefully, coming to a similar conclusion. In this way, we, each one of us, share the satisfaction which made Archimedes cry out in the excitement of discovery. It can be a religious experience. So much for the simple logic and the appreciation of granite. What remains are the mysteries or the calculated details which stretch credulity in even the most dedicated of geologists. Experimental work with the minerals of granite give some idea of the temperatures of crystallisation for a mineral such as feldspar, the most visible in the normal granite textures. A study of the effects of temperature, in turn, allows speculation as to the depths within the crust where crystallisation took place. From this comes the notion that granites formed, perhaps, some five miles below the surface of the crust – below 9,000 metres of cover rock which has subsequently been removed to allow granite to outcrop on the moor slopes above Castle Drogo. Other measurements made on granite assess the slow decay of radioactive minerals which change to lead at a measured and regular rate, giving us a geological 'clock' by which we can calculate the age of the intrusion of Dartmoor granite into the pre-existing killas and limestone. However difficult it may be to visualise five miles or 9,000 metres of depth, a date of 290 million years must take us into the incomprehensible. Perhaps we should leave it at that. After its formation, deep within the crust, granite was eventually exposed at the surface as a result of deep erosion; literally the 'gnawing away' of some 9,000 metres of cover, all of which must have been swept seawards down an antediluvian Teign Valley to form new rocks on a younger sea bed.

This brings us to the next chapter in the history of geology as a science. Early geologists like James Hutton have to be credited with another concept which remains vital to our science. This was a truly Greek appreciation that matter is never destroyed, but simply transferred to another place. If rocks decay, their debris accumulates, consolidates and ultimately forms new rock. The process is a cycle which they summarised with the phrase, '*in the economy of Nature, there is no vestige of a beginning, no prospect of an end*...'[1] So, how do granites decay and break down to create debris from which new rock can be created? Initially, we have to climb to the tors of the moor and recognise that those exposed hilltops often look like great cyclopean walls, squared block resting upon squared block like a scaled-up version of a moorland dry-stone wall. Little wonder that the moorland tors gave rise to legends of giants or the Devil pitching and scattering boulders of super-human scale. It may sound prosaic to be scientific but the apparently stacked blocks are really a record of the cooling history of the granite from an original molten form. Cooling was accompanied by contraction and the visible cracks are shrinkage pull-aparts, called 'joints' by geologists. Subsequently exposed to wind, rain and frost, the same joints are exploited by weathering, opened up to the extent that squared masses detach themselves and slide, under gravity, to create a block scree – for which the local name, 'clitter', seems thoroughly appropriate – a clutter of granite blocks which, at a distance, look for all the world like a static flock of grey sheep. Gravity and the slopes of the moor edge naturally take house-sized clitter downslope into the streams, periodically aided by the lubricating effect of Dartmoor rains. One of the most awe-inspiring experiences can be the sight and sound of a moorland stream in flood. Stones of considerable size can be shifted bodily by surges of water already carrying pebbles and boulders as an armament. The accompanying noise can be quite horrendous. Strangely, the power of moving water to break up and transport rock was not, at first, evident to the early geologists. Their view, often, was that valleys and gorges were the result of fissures opening up in the ground as a consequence of earthquakes or folding movements. By the early nineteenth century, however, running water was recognised as the commonest of the agents of erosion, moulding and fashioning the landscape more or less constantly under our regime of climate.

If you have followed this so far, you will appreciate that the boulder in the stream bed, which catches the eye of Peter Randall-Page and appeals to his imagination for what it might become when cut, manipulated and crafted, has already passed through several significant stages of natural process. It reveals several of the fundamental principles of the science of geology and continues to provoke thought upon the origins of the crust, the cycle of erosion, and the permanence of matter. William Blake saw the world in a grain of sand; Charles Kingsley traced the tale of a pebble; the history of a clitter boulder can be just as profound. The sculpture, *Granite Song*, goes that bit further by blurring the boundaries between art and science – if we ever thought to separate them.

[1] James Hutton, *Theory of the Earth,* 1795

# PASSAGE 1992

Dartmoor granite and lead
125 x 163 x 119cm, 125 x 163 x 127cm

Located at the end of an avenue of mature trees, on either side of a gap in a stone wall, in Whiddon Deer Park (National Trust) between Chagford and Drewsteignton.
OS map ref. SX725895

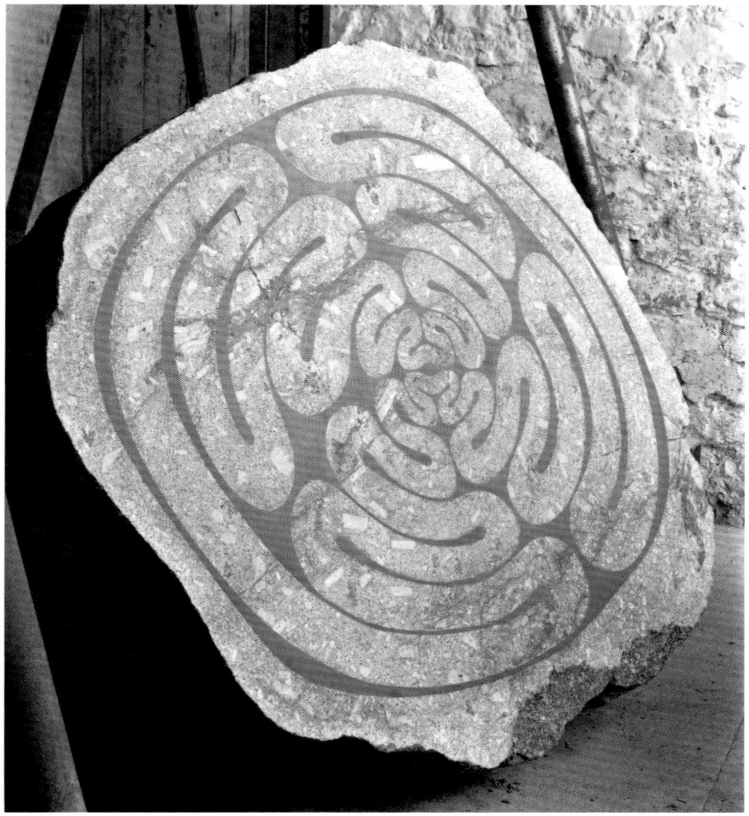

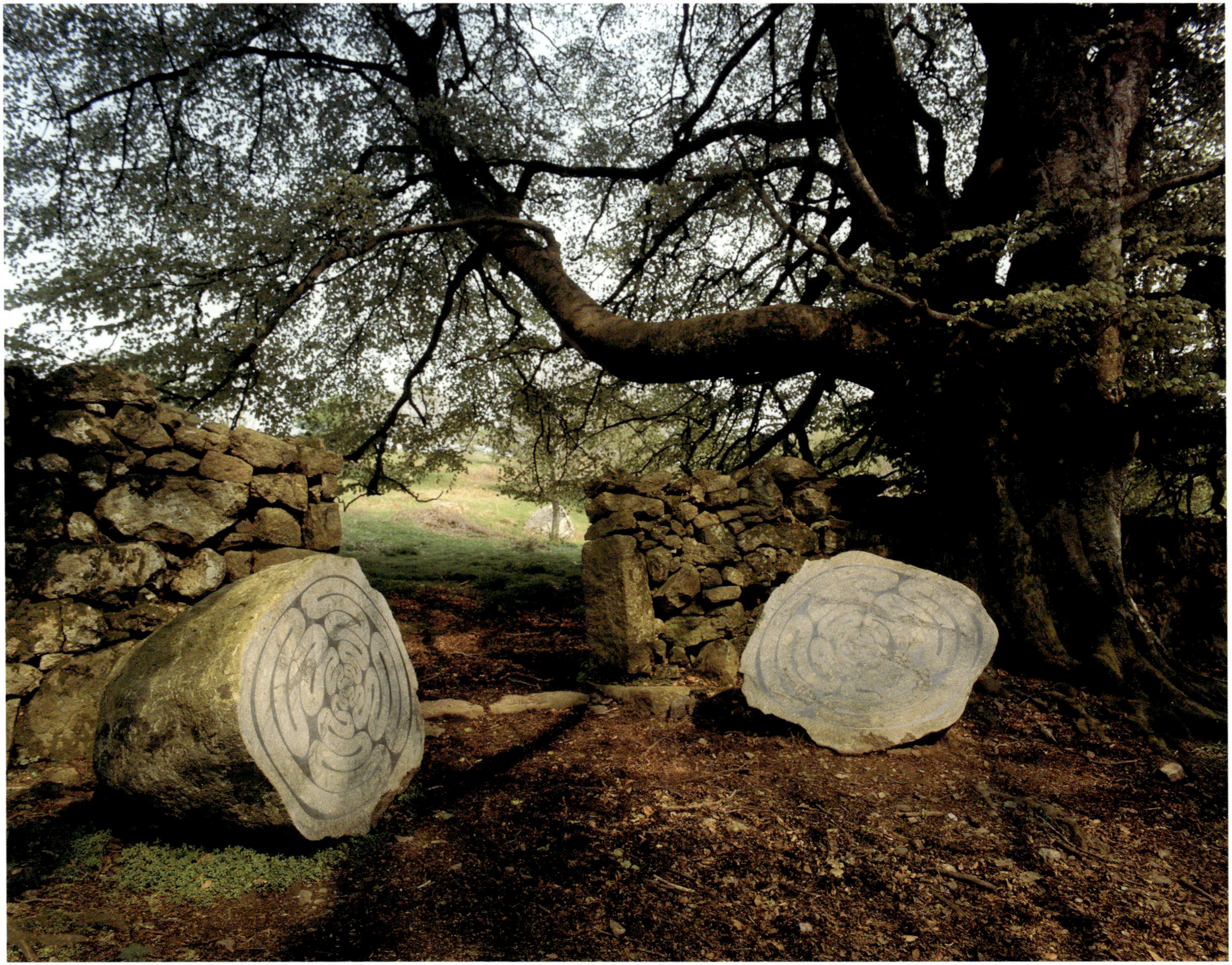

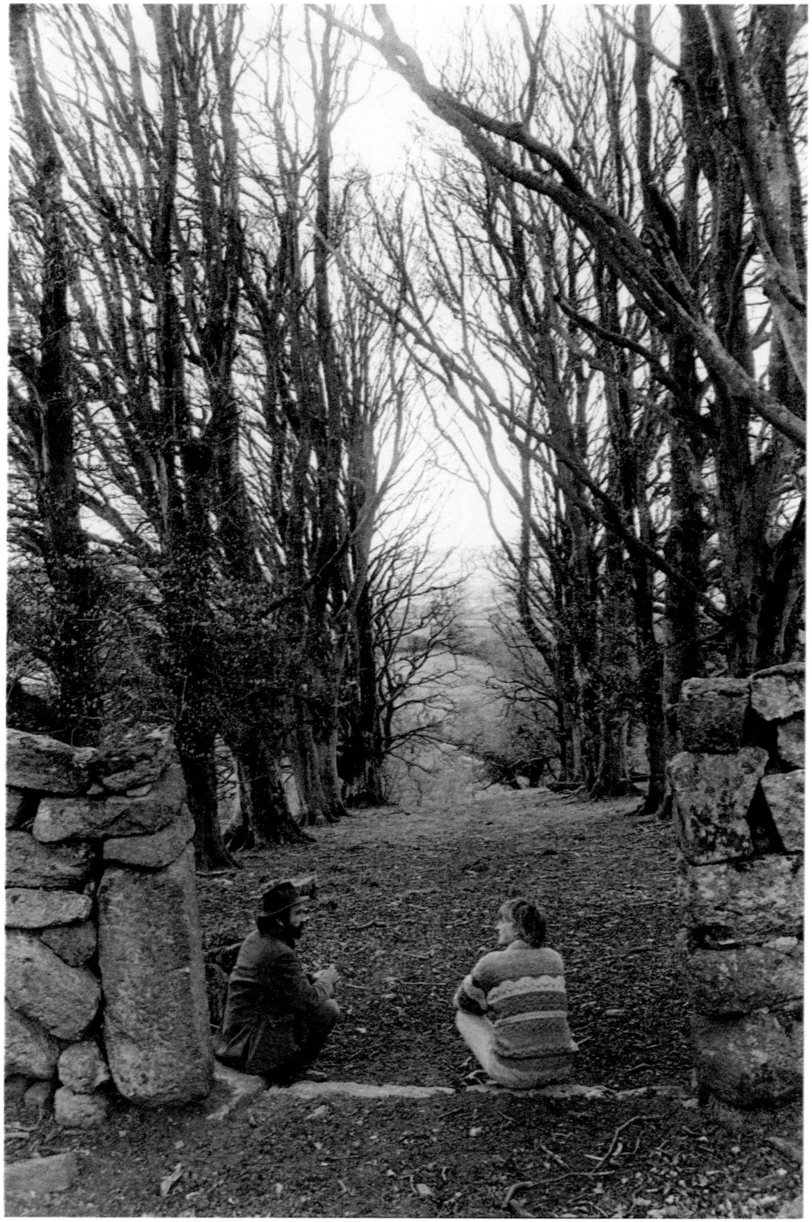

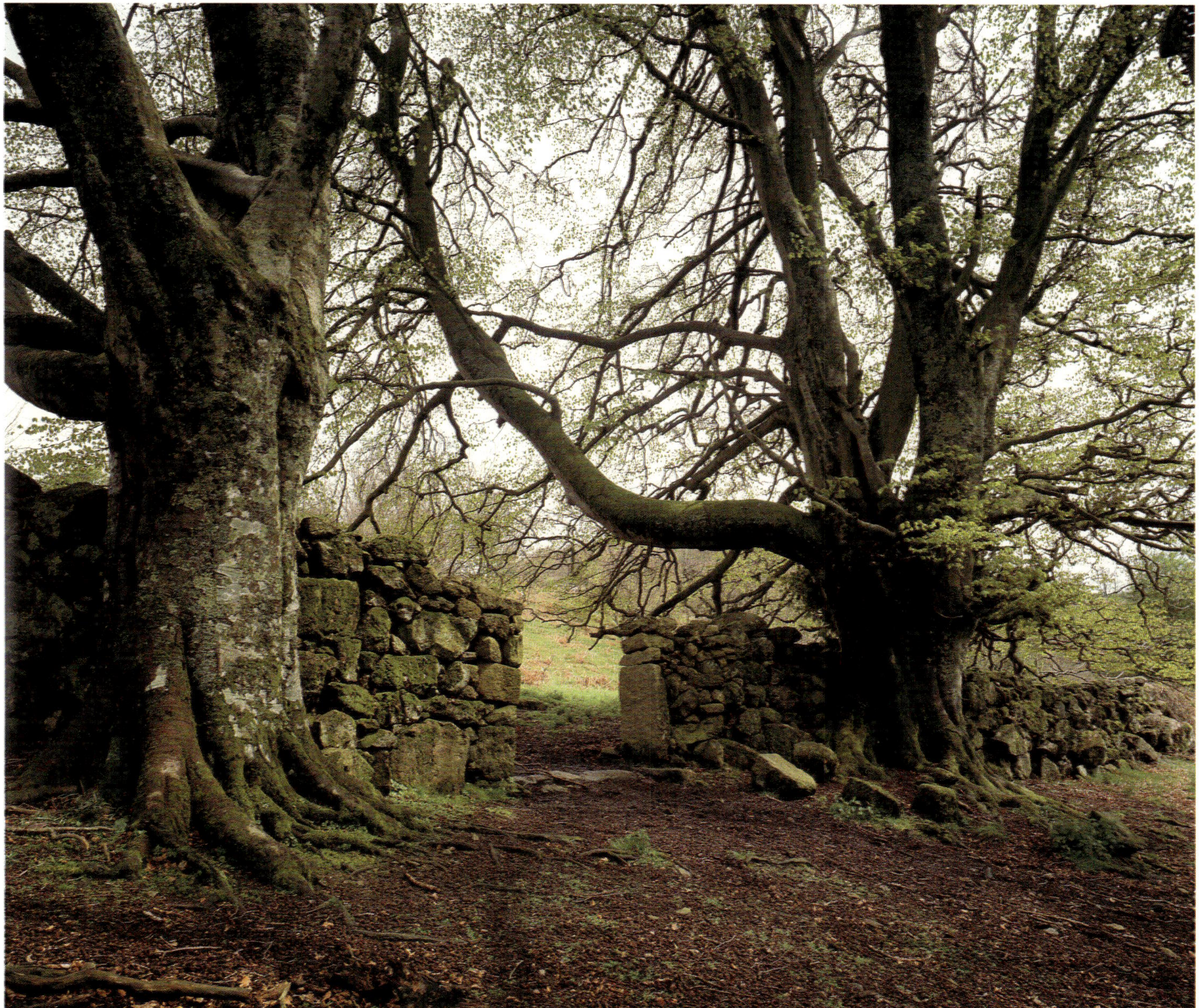

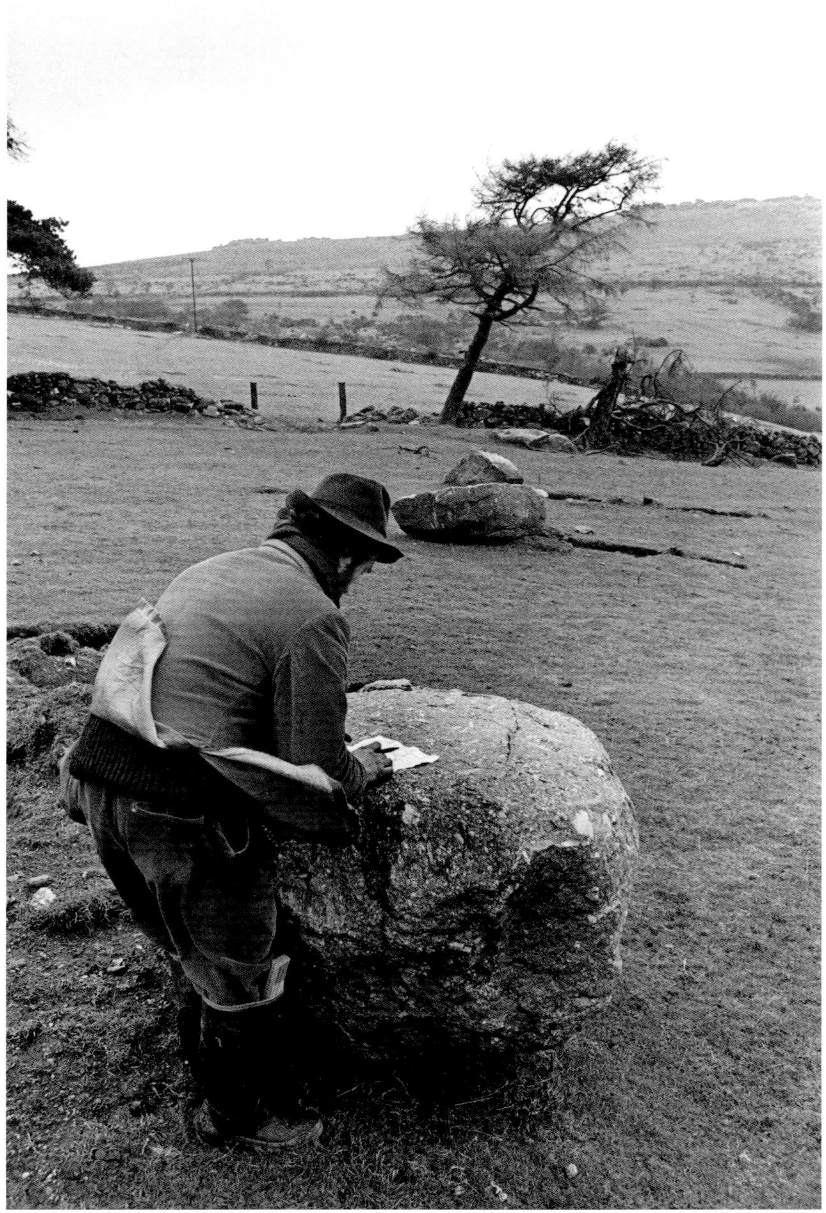

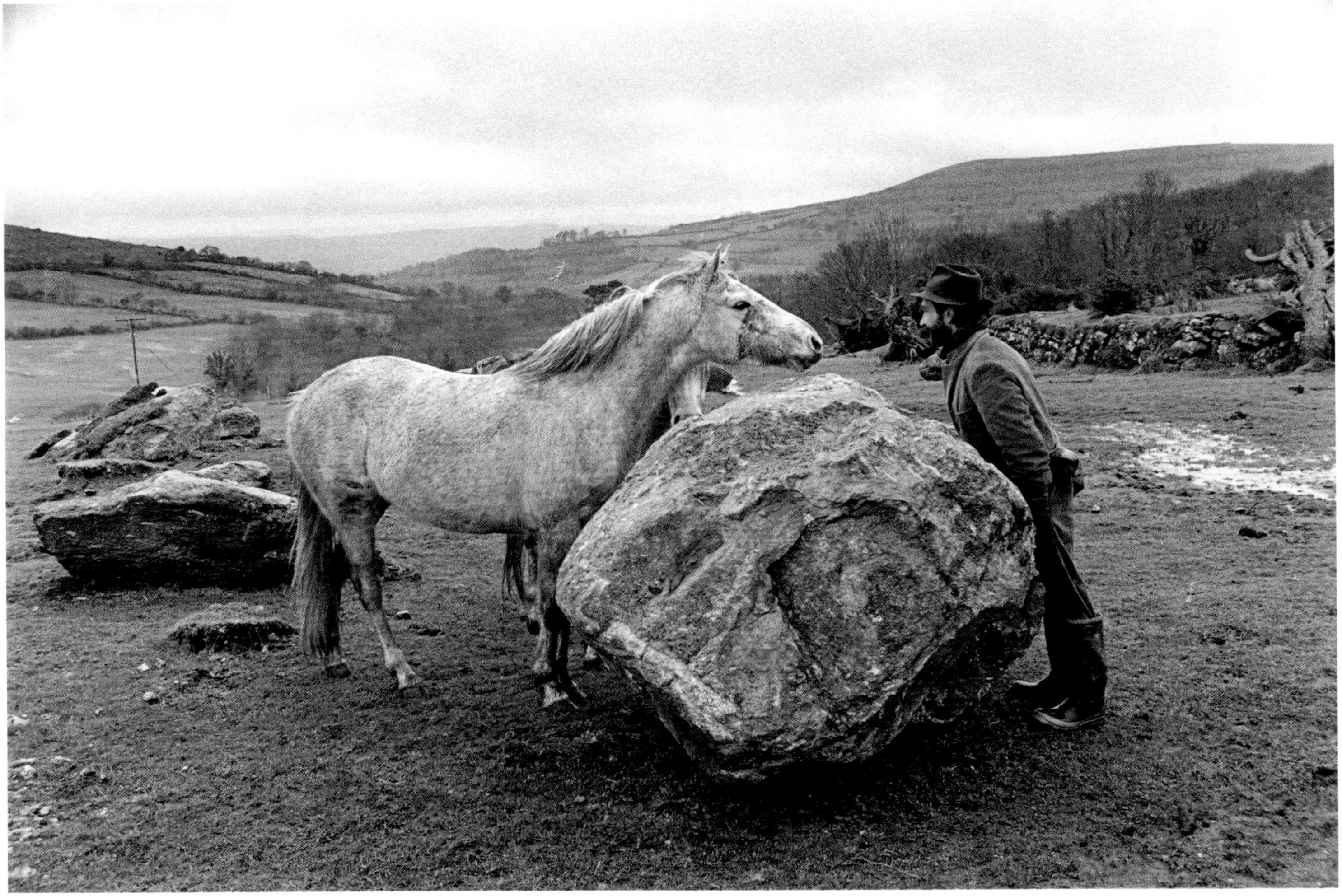

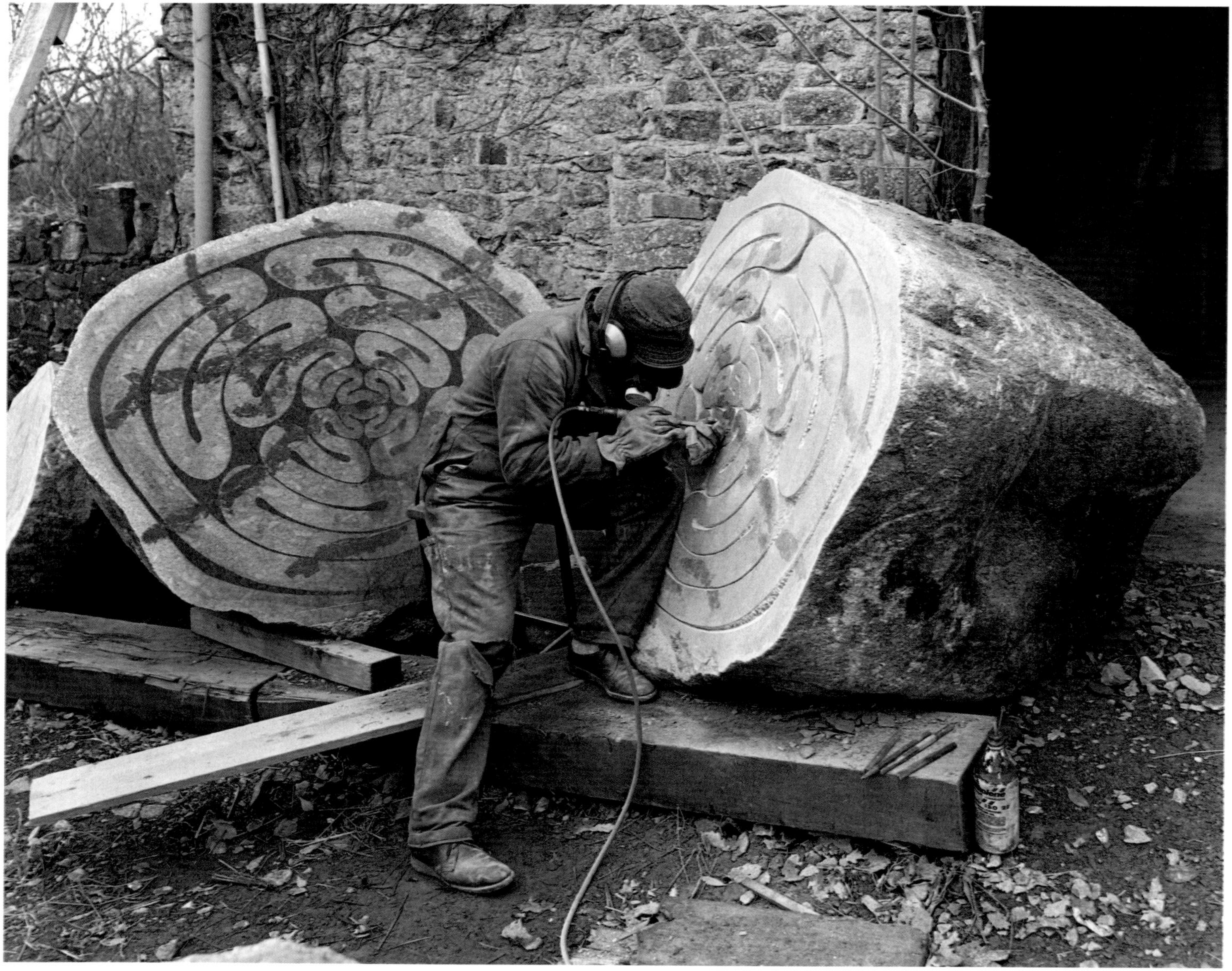

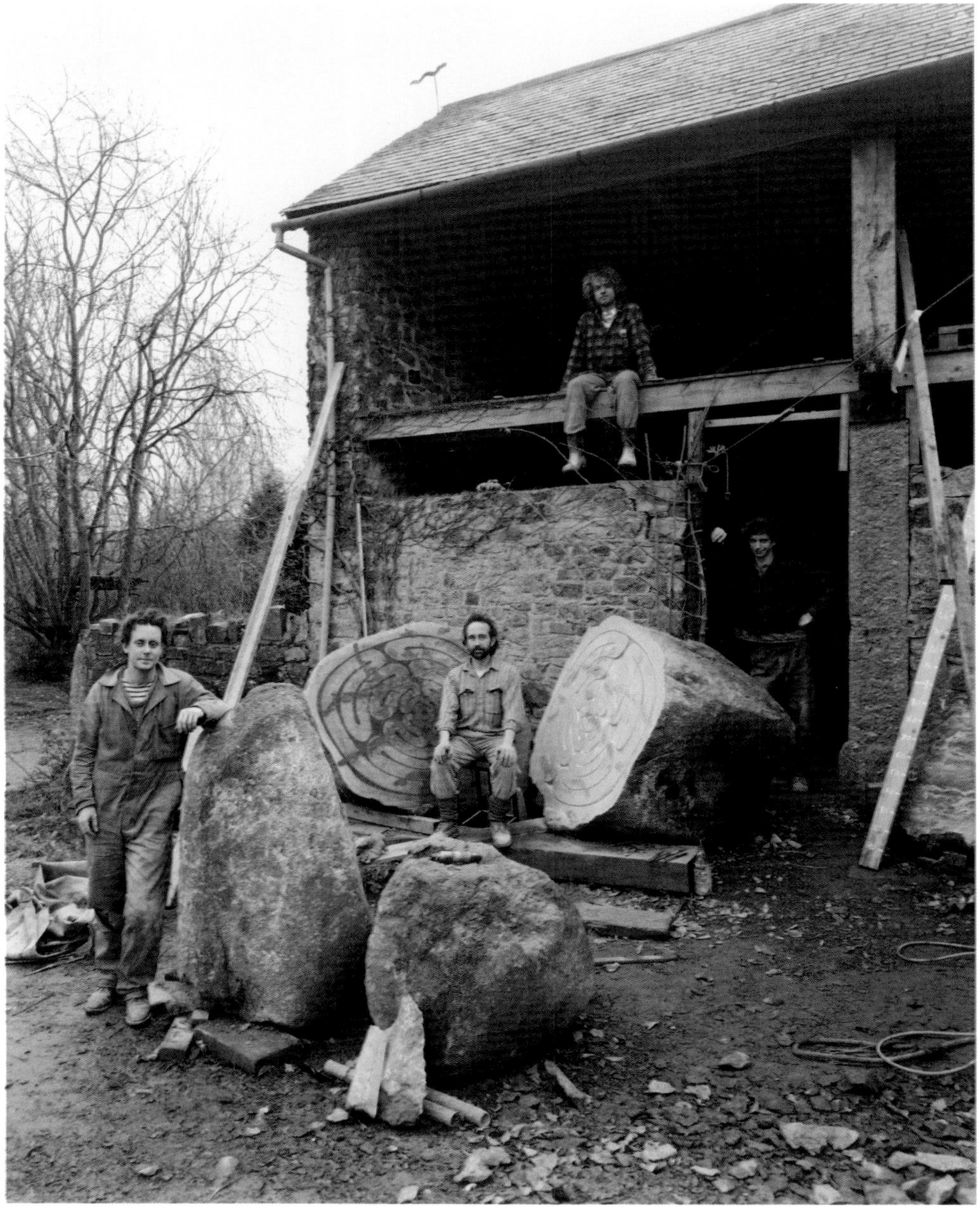

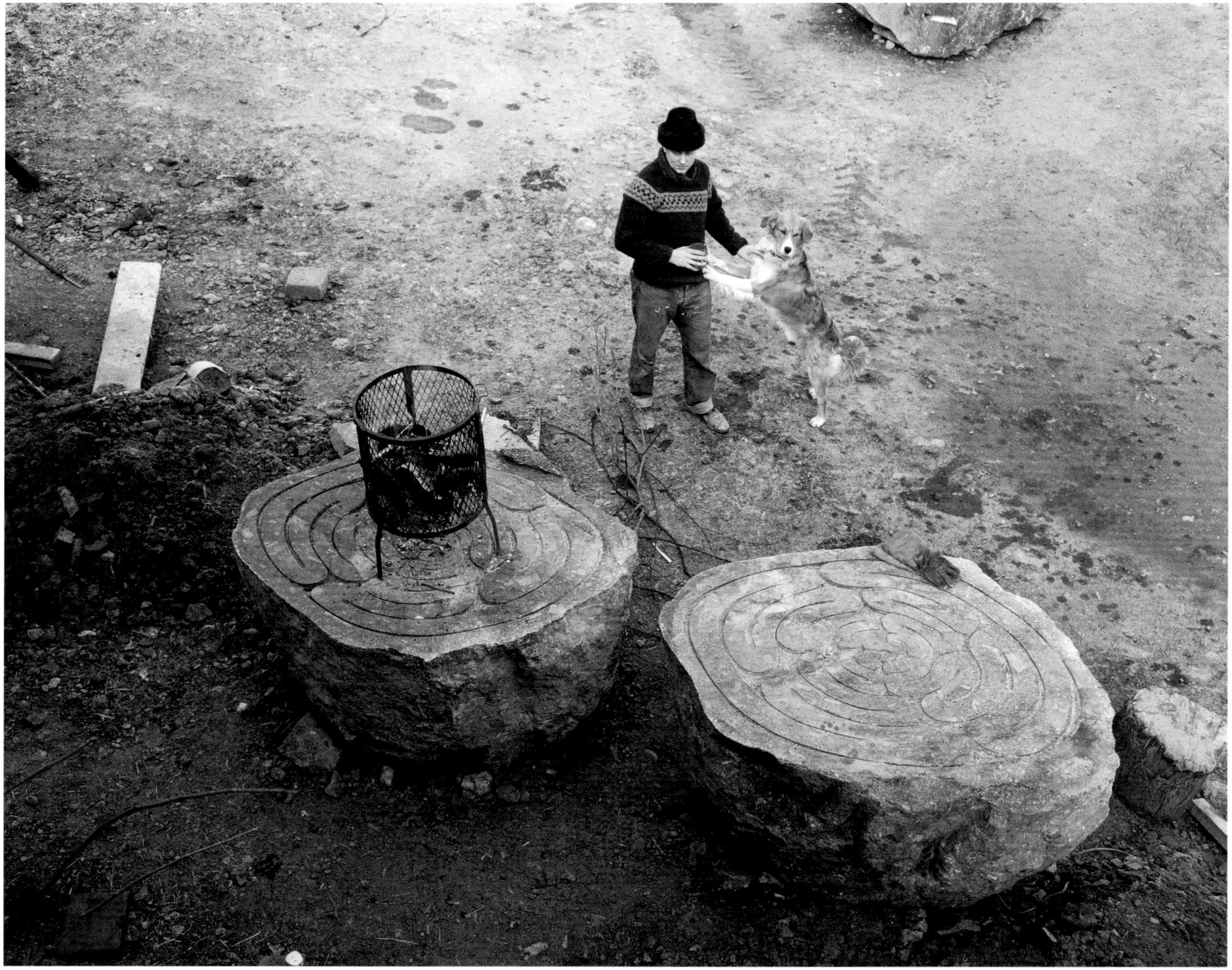

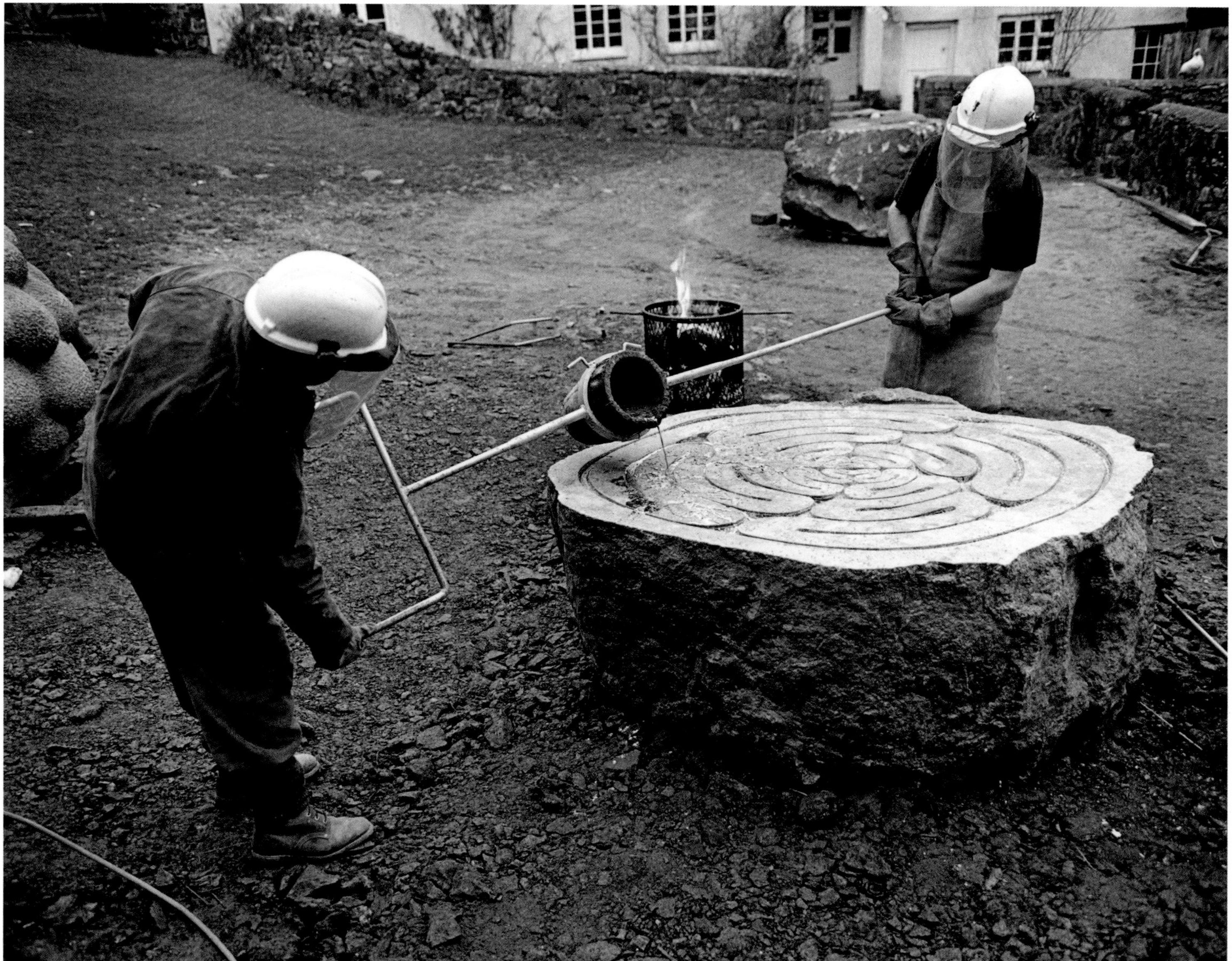

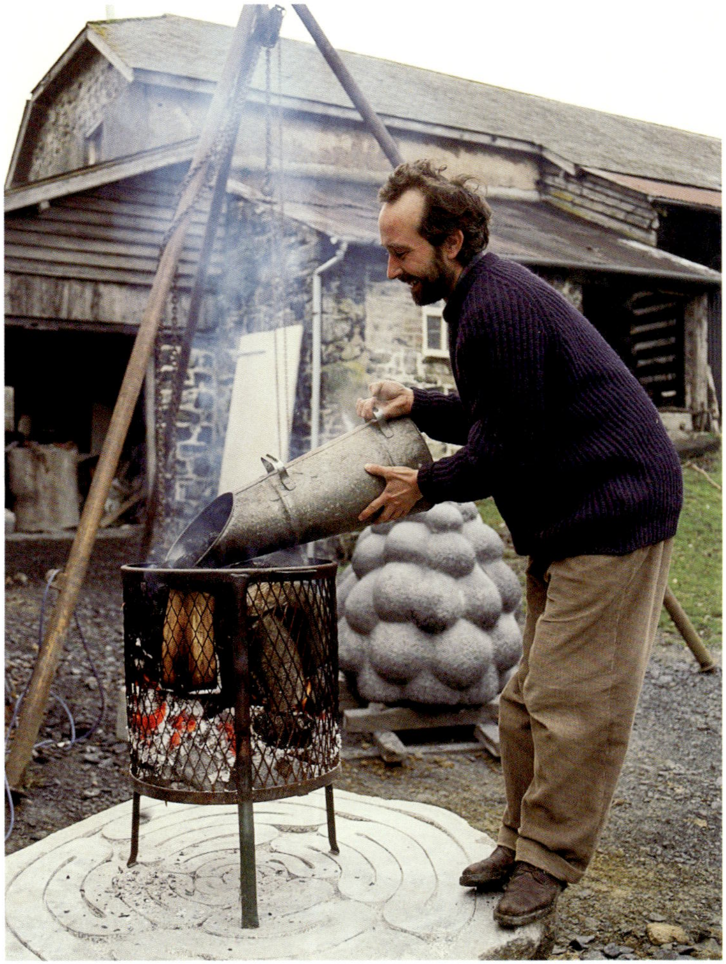

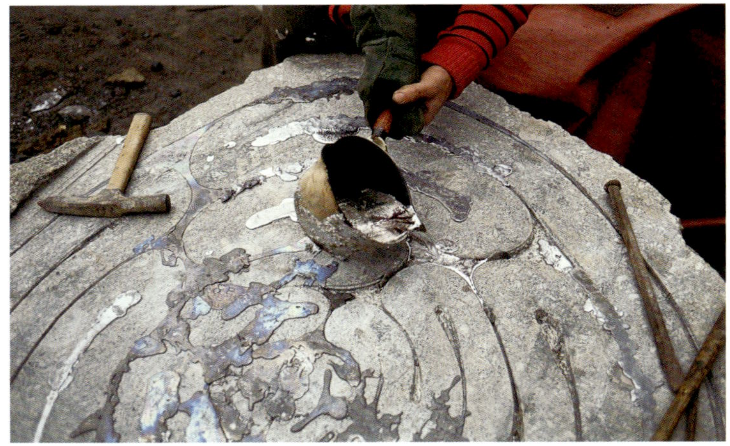

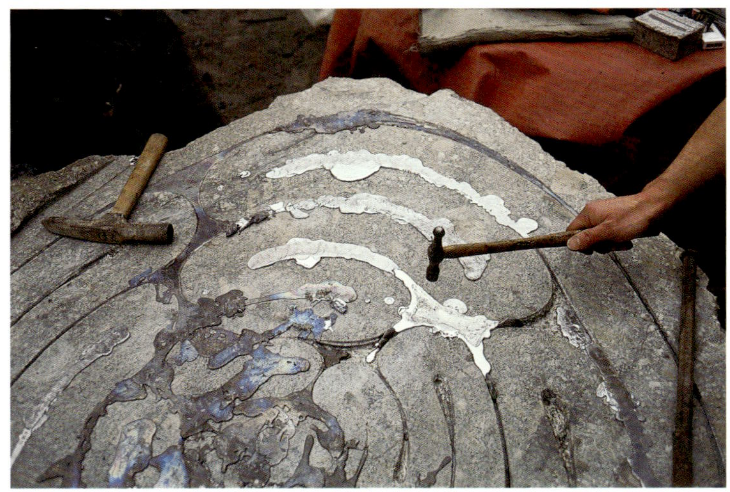

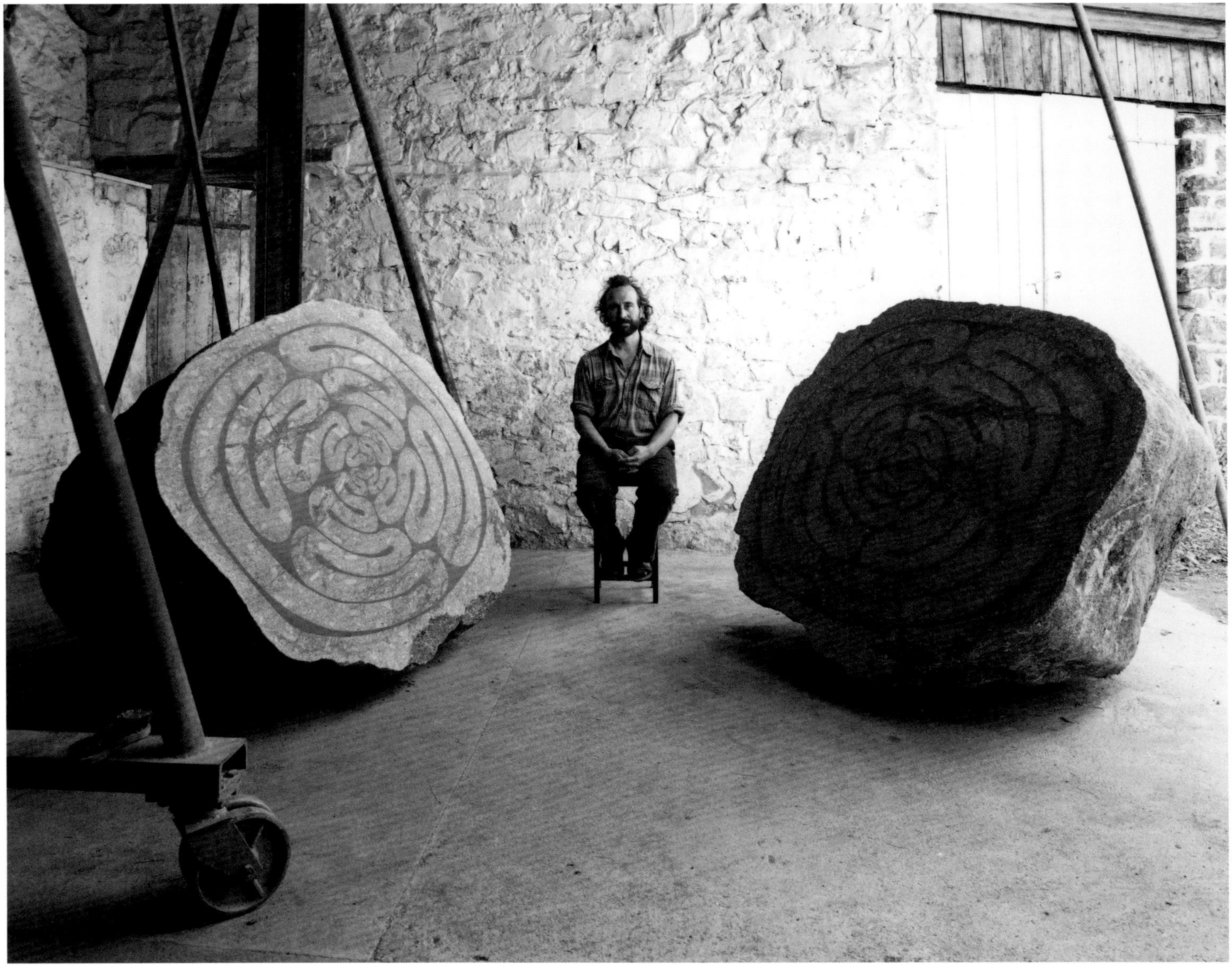

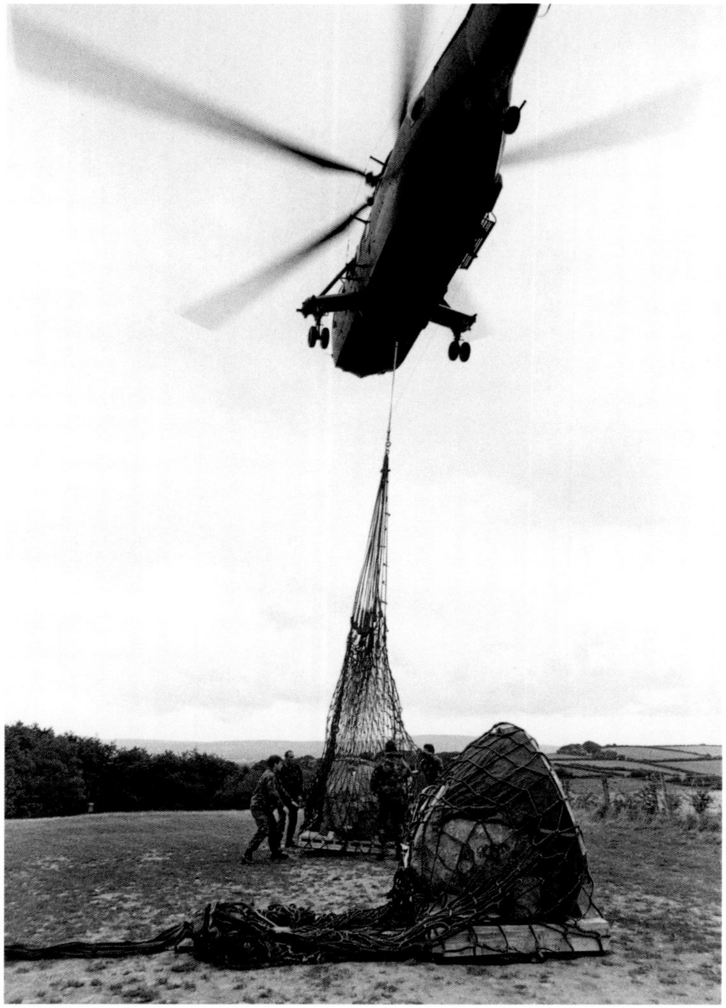

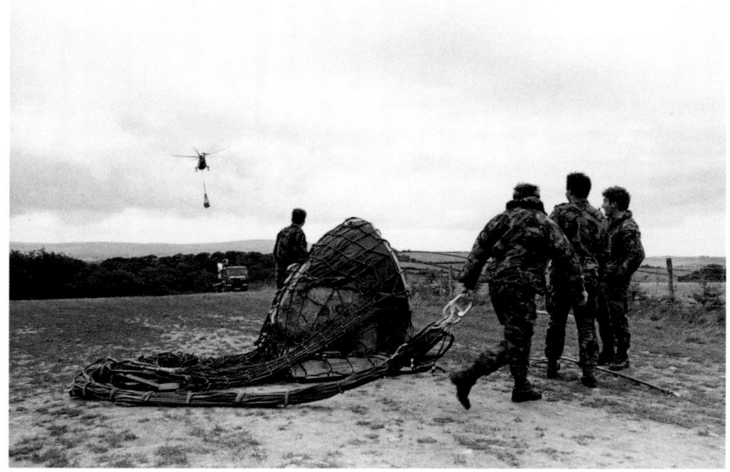

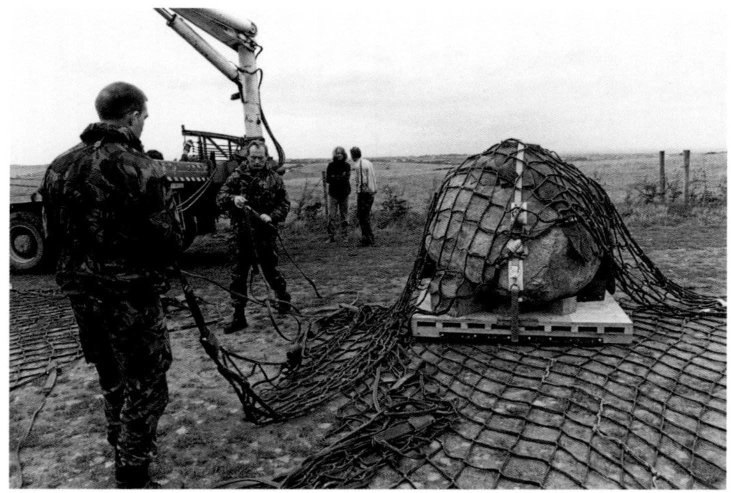

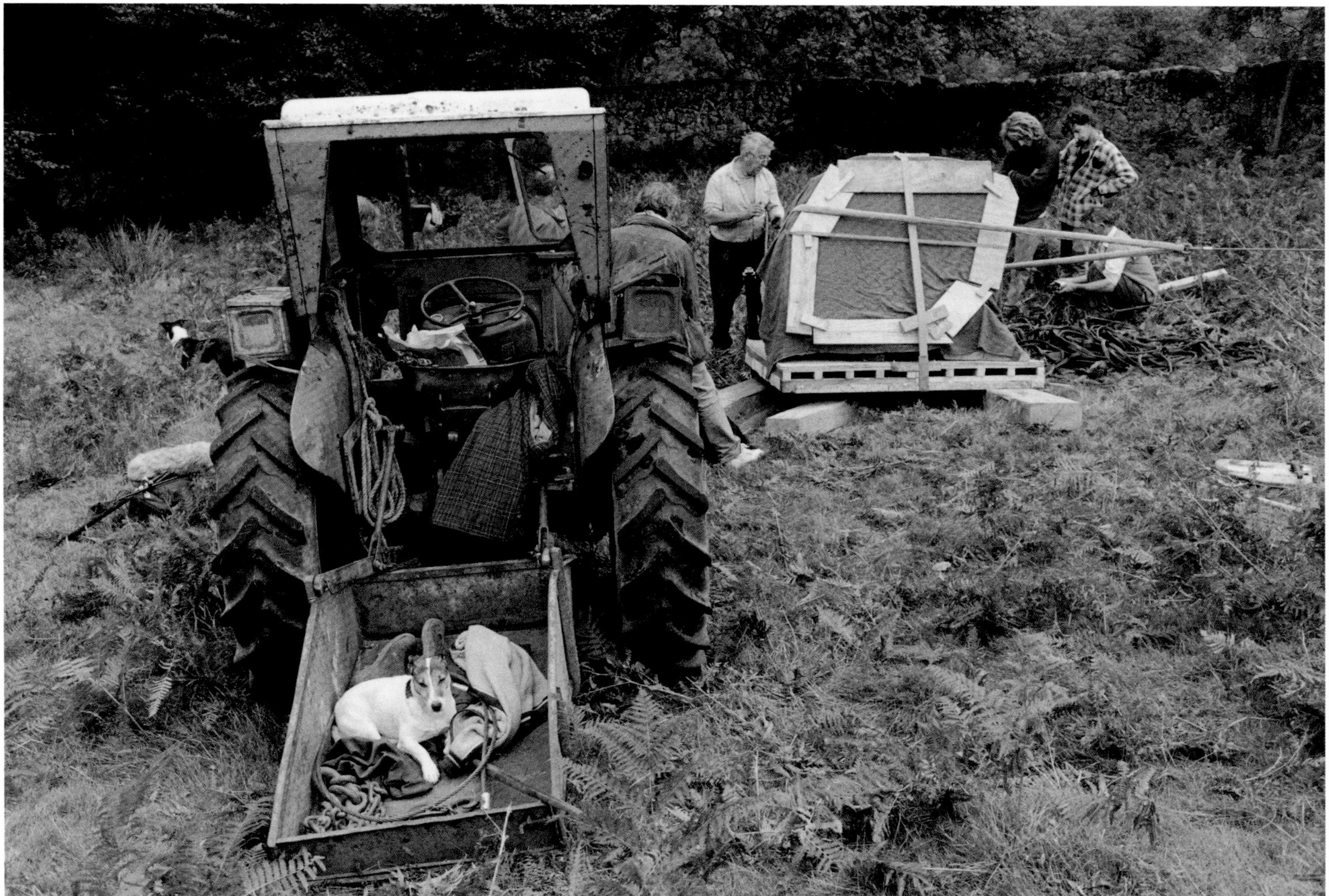

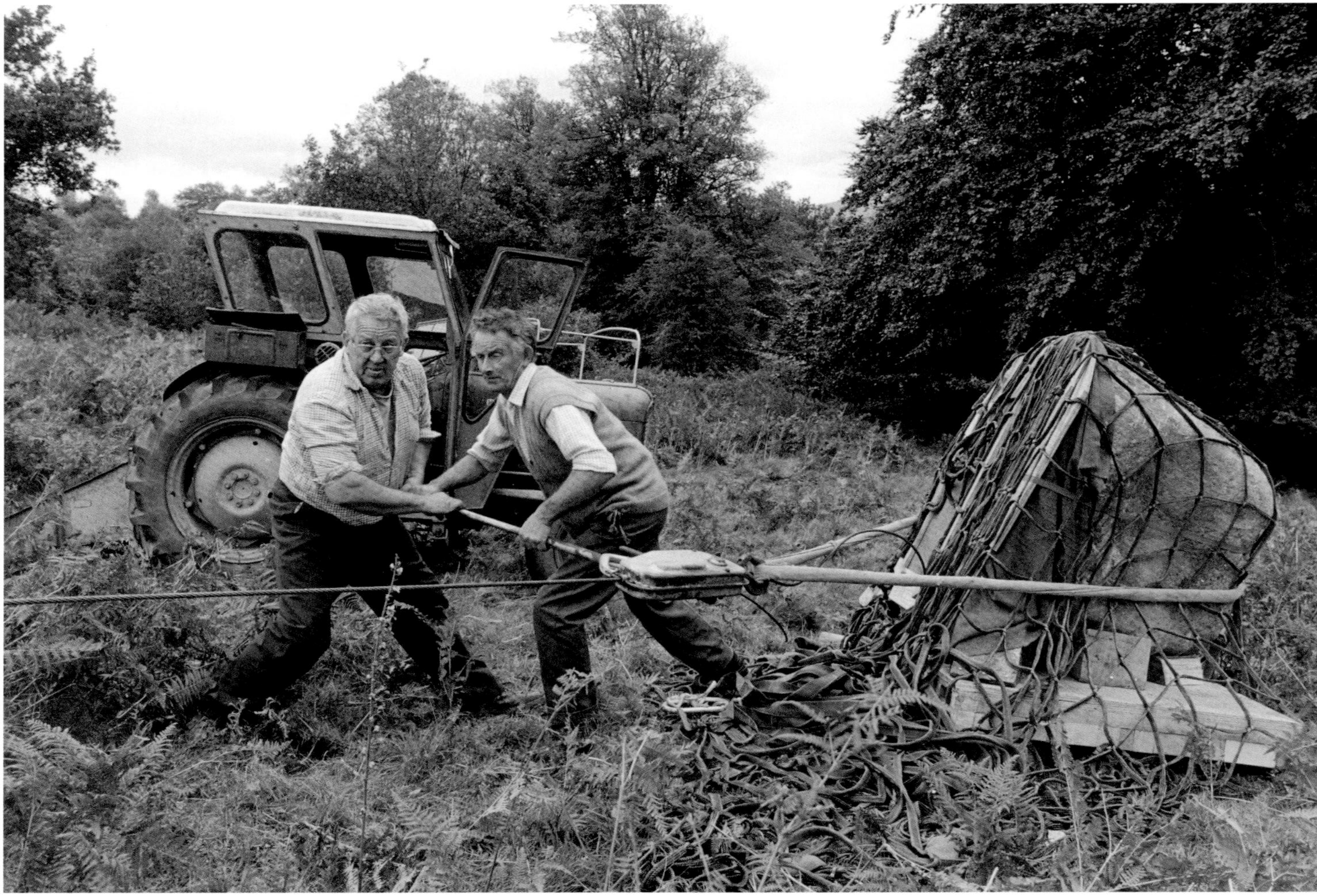

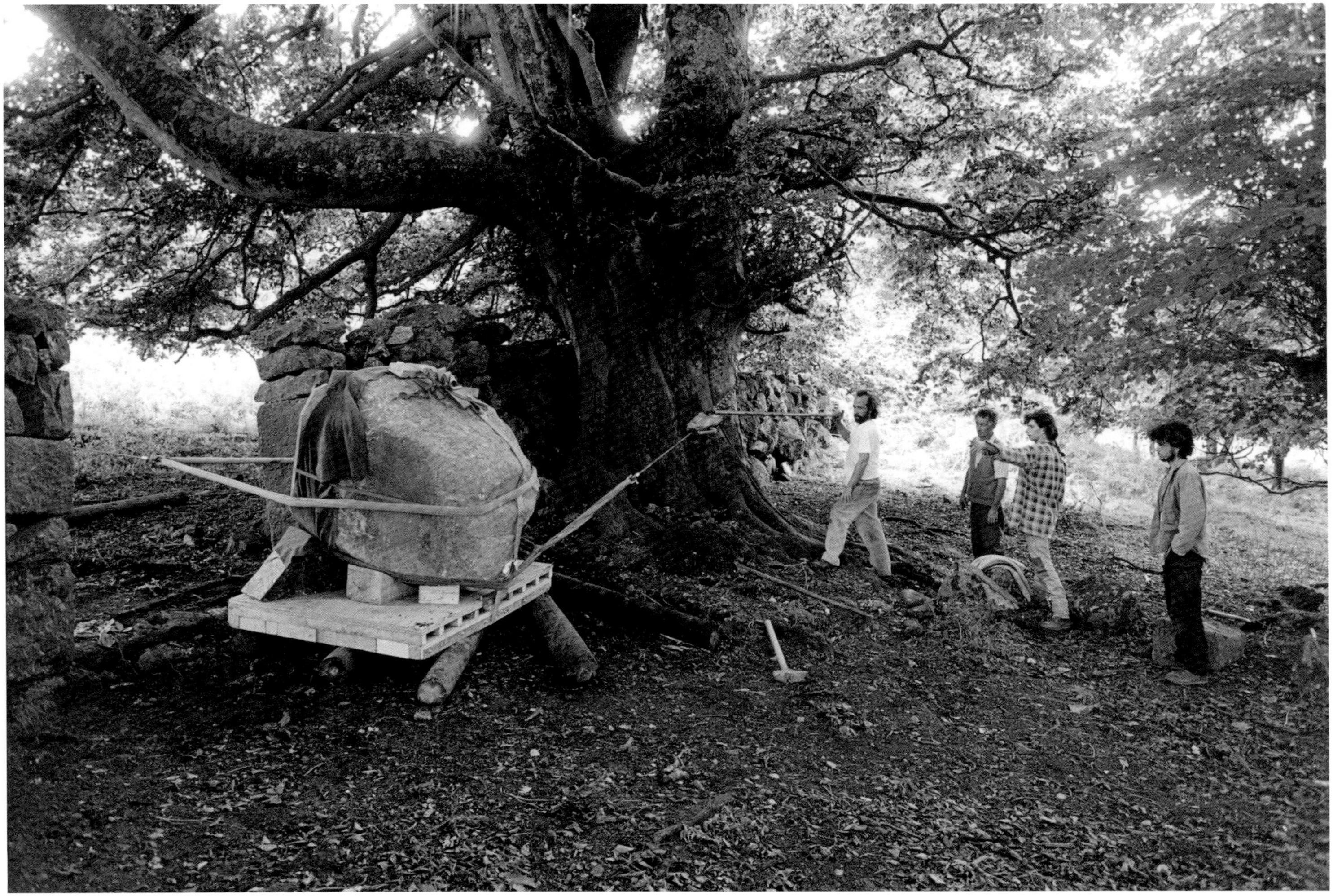

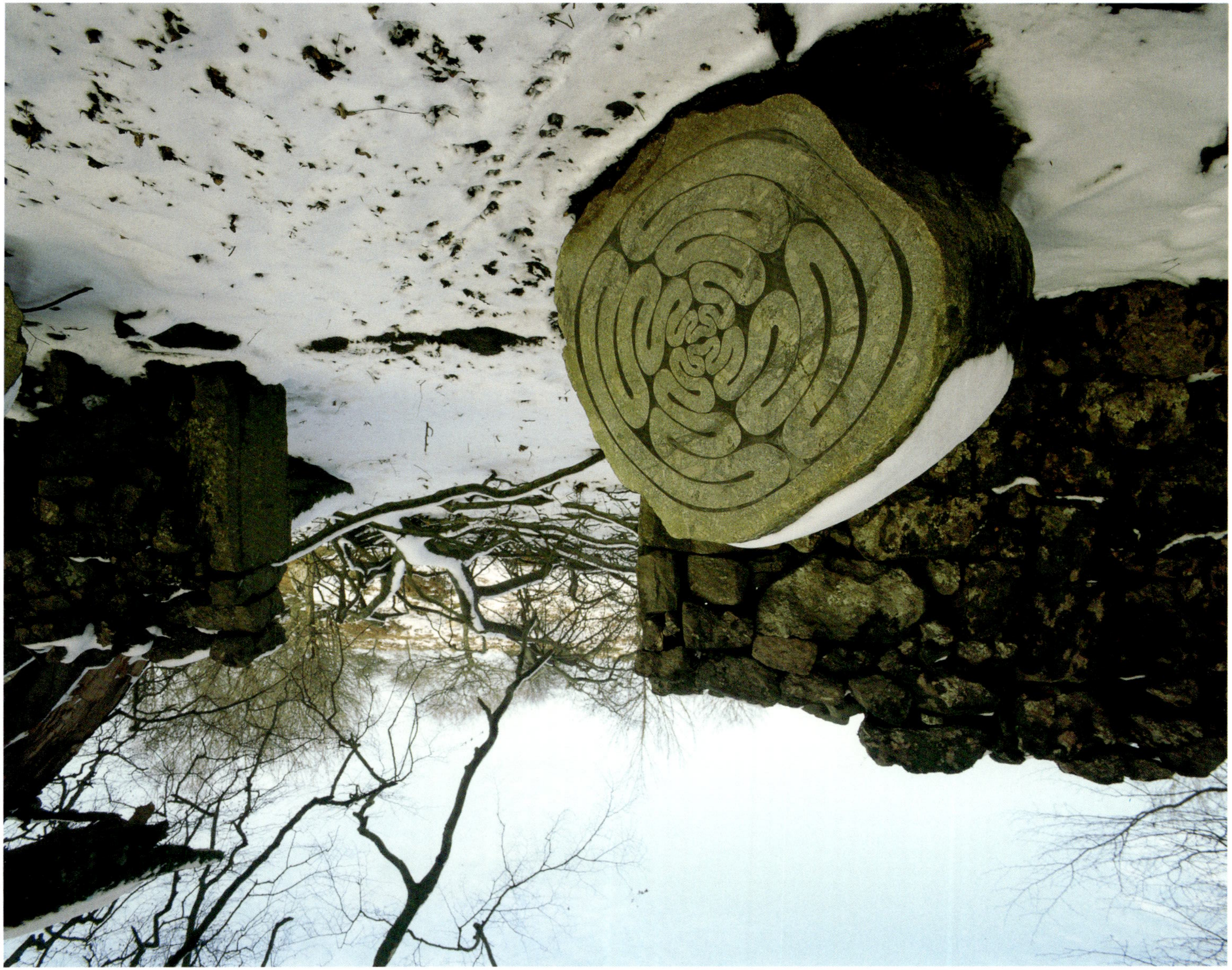

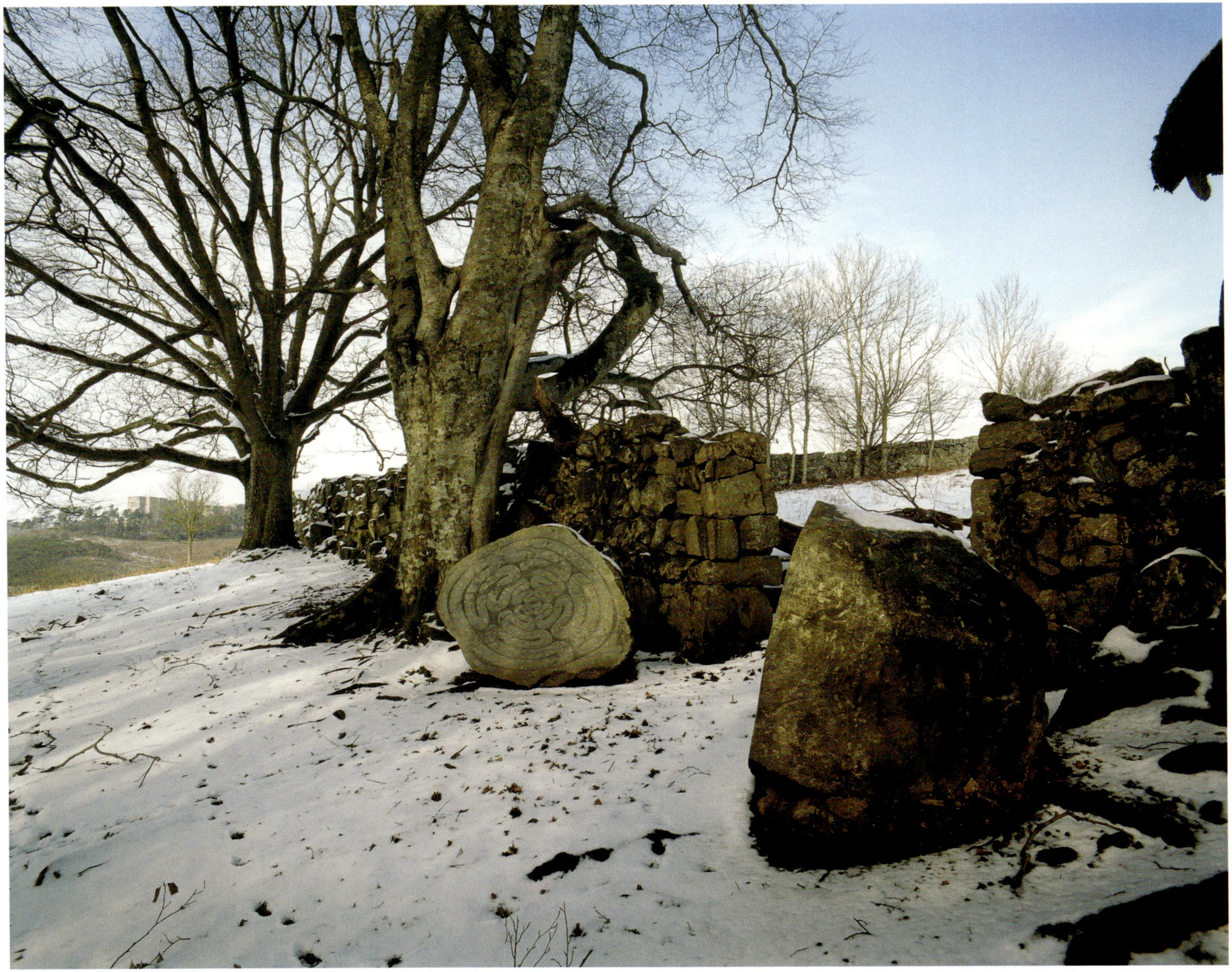

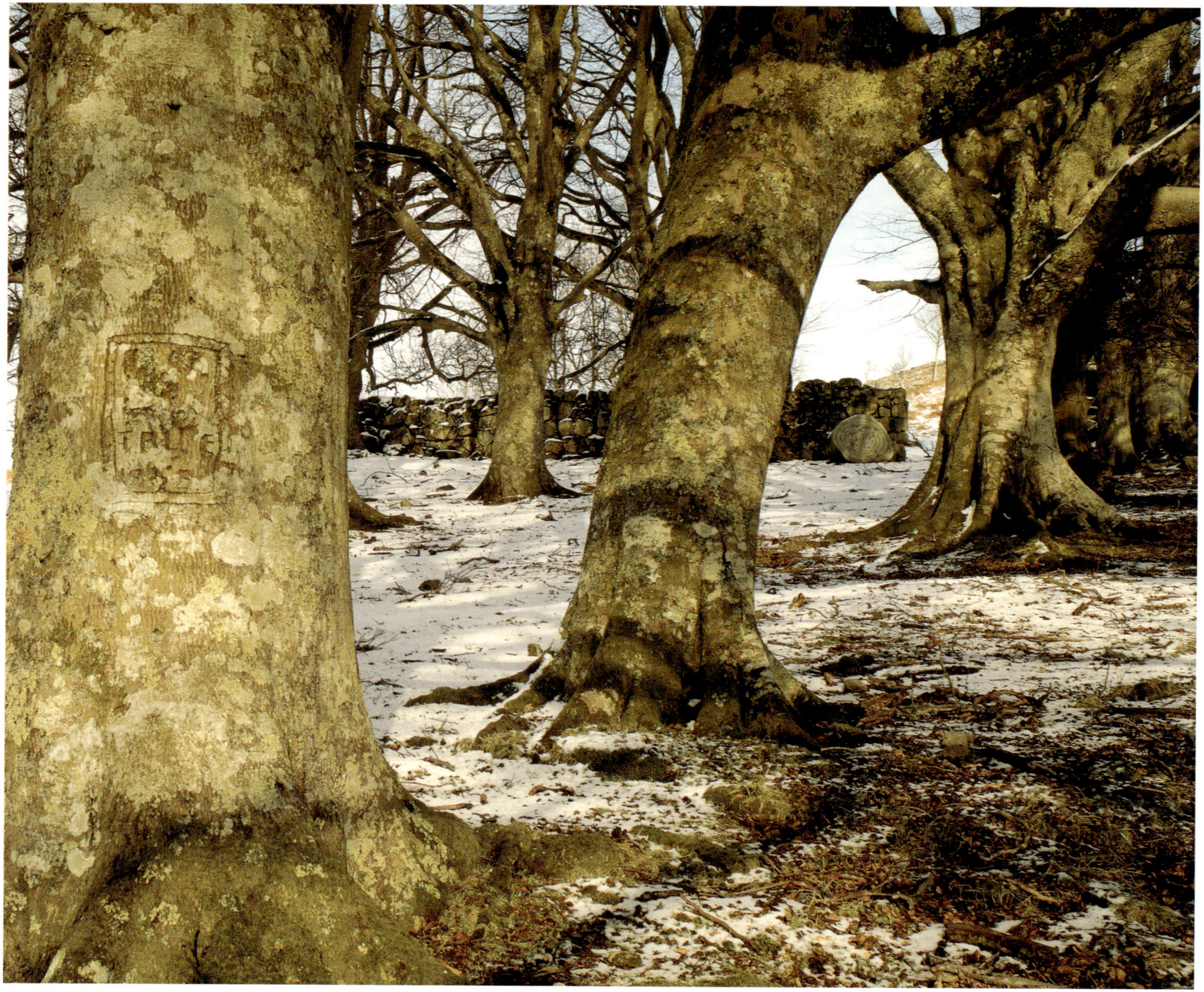

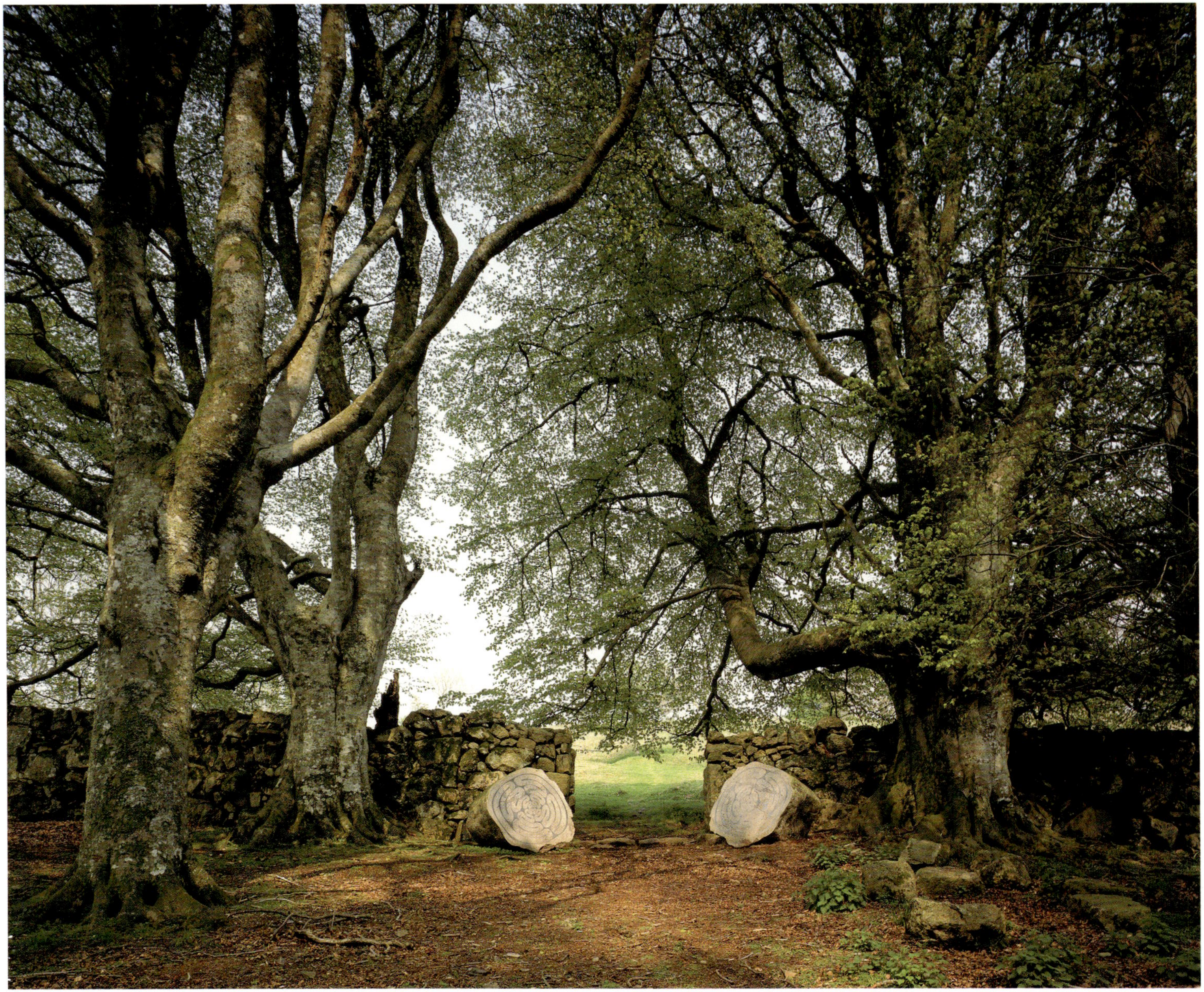

## IMAGINING FUTURE MEMORIES

Sue Clifford and Angela King, Common Ground

The youth dragged his feet, or kicked at rocks. His parents, some way in front, were unselfconsciously tapping, gasping and grinning at fossils unlocked from eons of entrapment. Bored, infuriated, excruciated, he rehearsed the dance of separation. '*They are nothing to do with me... I don't want to be here*'. At his feet, a stone, like all the rest lapped by the salty tide, spoke to him. He stared at the words upon it. A twinge of fear, he glanced across to mother/father: regression – momentary – a tug of safety. Comforted, he again looked down. The stone still spoke. Alternately scanning the whole beach and staring down, he lingered and, after a while, smiling, he walked on thoughtfully but purposefully.

We were some way away from him on Charmouth beach. We had brought back the heavy stone across which Richard Grasby had so beautifully carved 'Common Ground'. This was no holiday, we wanted photographs of the stone amongst its peers, beside the cliffs, to show what we are, what we believe in. It would be good to hear his version of the story, but it manifestly gave him pause, and we shall never forget it.

It is possible to intervene in a place and to add to its richness. It is possible to help people see and feel things they might never have confronted.

Nature works relentlessly on her *'grand projets'*, we have been fellow travellers in these islands for a few thousand years. It has been constant work, forging city and country, virtually no stone is without our mark, although we persist in believing that, in the country is nature, and in the city is culture.

Common Ground works to excite people's curiosity about the variegated conspiracies of culture with nature which makes 'places', to value the richnesses of the everyday, to savour the symbolisms with which we have endowed nature, to revalue our emotional engagement with places and all that they mean to us, and to go on to become actively involved in their future. Through our work on Local Distinctiveness, we have tried to liberate us all from the preoccupation with the beautiful, the rare and the spectacular to help people explore, express and savour what makes the commonplace particular.

Places are not just physical surroundings – they are a web of rich, evolving understandings between people and nature, peoples and their histories, people and their neighbours. And they are to be found in dense city, haphazard suburb and wide country.

Most people understand places and value them because they mean something to them. Small things (detail) and overlapping clues to previous lives and landscapes (patina) may be the very things which breathe significance into the streets or fields. Try to define these things from the outside or at a grand scale and the point is lost.

Local Distinctiveness is also about accommodation and change, about accumulations and assemblages, not about preservation and compartmentalisation. A local culture which has sufficient self knowledge, identity and self esteem, is confident in welcoming new people and new ideas and it knows its invisible assets as well as the apparent: symbol, festival, legend, custom, language, recipe, memory.

But much activity – development, farming – has reduced variegation producing uniformity in housing, high streets, factories, fields which could be anywhere, and removing the subtle things which help people 'own' the place through familiarity. Some change removes everything that has gone before.

As we have explained elsewhere, the forces of homogenisation rob us of visible and invisible things which have meaning to us, they devalue our longitudinal wisdom and erase fragments from which to piece together the stories of nature and history through which our humanity is fed. They stunt our sensibilities and starve our imagination. And, as Bachelard has said, '*imagination separates us from the past as well as reality, it faces the future. If we cannot imagine, we cannot foresee.*'[1]

[1] *Local Distinctiveness: Place, Particularity and Identity;* Common Ground, 1993.

We believe that we shall need all of the social imagination and humanity we can muster to face the complexities of the future.

In encouraging Peter Randall-Page to carefully intervene in his own surroundings (and we would have worked with him in Camden Town in the middle of London had he still lived there), the prospect was not simply to release sculpture into the wild, but to demonstrate that powerful provocation to revalue the ordinary things of this place – a boulder, a wall, a spring – can come from subtle pointers.

Common Ground's work wanders through the realms of building, archaeology, history, ecology, landscape, planning, horticulture, farming, cooking, as well as music, poetry, painting. We work to encourage the weaving and reweaving of culture and nature, to inspire people with the richness of involvement in all of the dimensions of everyday places.

Peter's work is part of this, in the same way as that of the farmer who has kept Devon Reds for fifty years; it is as important as the woman working to create new uses for local orchard fruit; it ranks with the wallers who have come after a gap of three generations to re-erect a storm torn hedge bank; it adds power to the place like the mill, the quarry, May Day.

All of the works are beside footpaths, those wonderful lines of history which we must continue to draw in the land. Walking is a way of reconnecting, the pace and proximity makes thinking and talking so much easier. The excitement of finding something which simply makes you look more closely at everything else, provokes eddies of conversations and curiosity, feeds the imagination. Primroses, brick bonds, local beer, carved rocks can all engage us in different ways.

The sculptures are part of the dynamic of the place, part of the new. But they are already absorbed, lichens and mosses, peculiar to the area, know how to deal with local granite, hard as it is, and somehow, popular appreciation has embraced a touchstone. In the very first week after *Granite Song* had been settled into its islet in the river Teign, two different people told stories of how the boulder, which they had seen all their lives, had suddenly opened to reveal an intricate organic shape: the local mythmakers had already embraced and enhanced the work. Somehow, Peter Randall-Page had reached into the soul of the place, feeding unspoken musings of the secrets locked inside the boulders of these moors, fields and streams. A new myth emerging hardly metamorphosed, some deep connective memory, hope or imagining.

Somewhere remains a place because its people share in the retelling of its stories, teach each other to read its subtle cues, understand their significances, feel relaxed in its physical forms, find it easy to congregate, but the point is that, ordinary or special, a place holds an accumulation of meanings. The city and the country parish remain vital through absorption and reinvention. Local Distinctiveness is about the continual momentum of social memory, about meaning conveyed and reworked, helping us to feel part of the everyday, and unselfconscious contributors to continuing history.

It is perfectly possible that, in two thousand years' time, the Teign will have pushed *Granite Song* downstream, to be discovered one day by a boy, dragging his feet, bored and excruciated . . .

## BURROW STONE 1994

Granite
70 x 48 x 30cm

Located on a public footpath from Drewsteignton to Burrow Farm.
OS map ref. SX747910

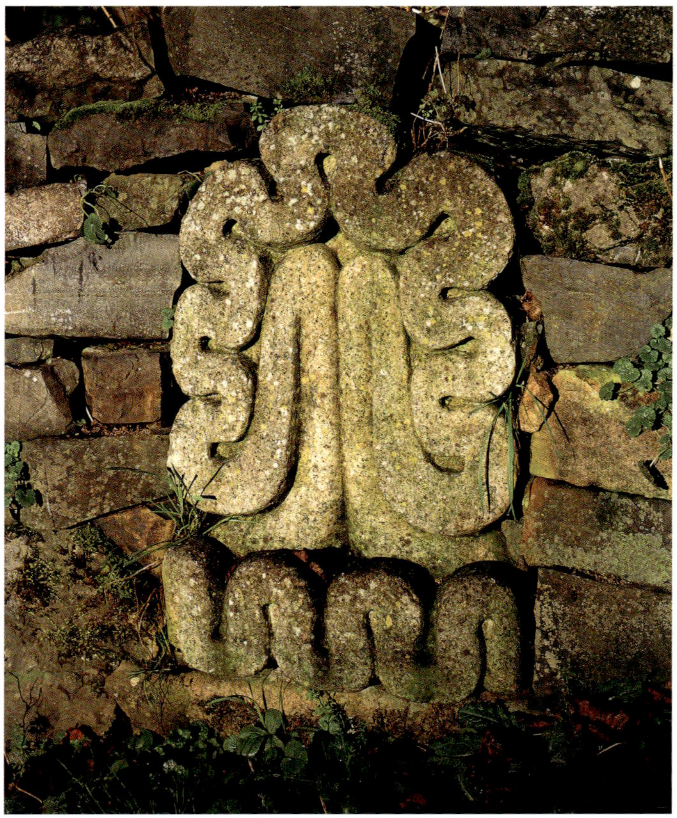

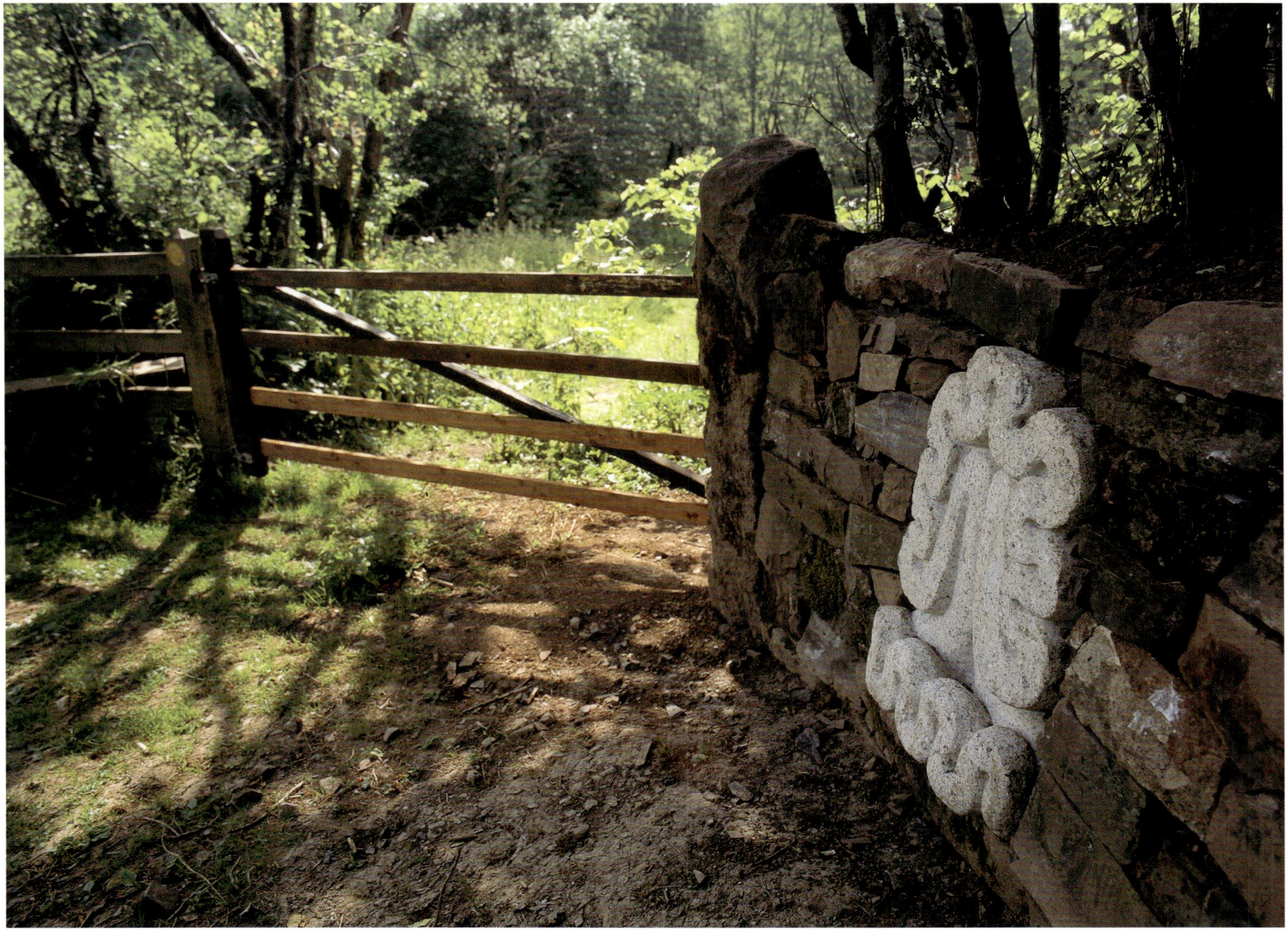

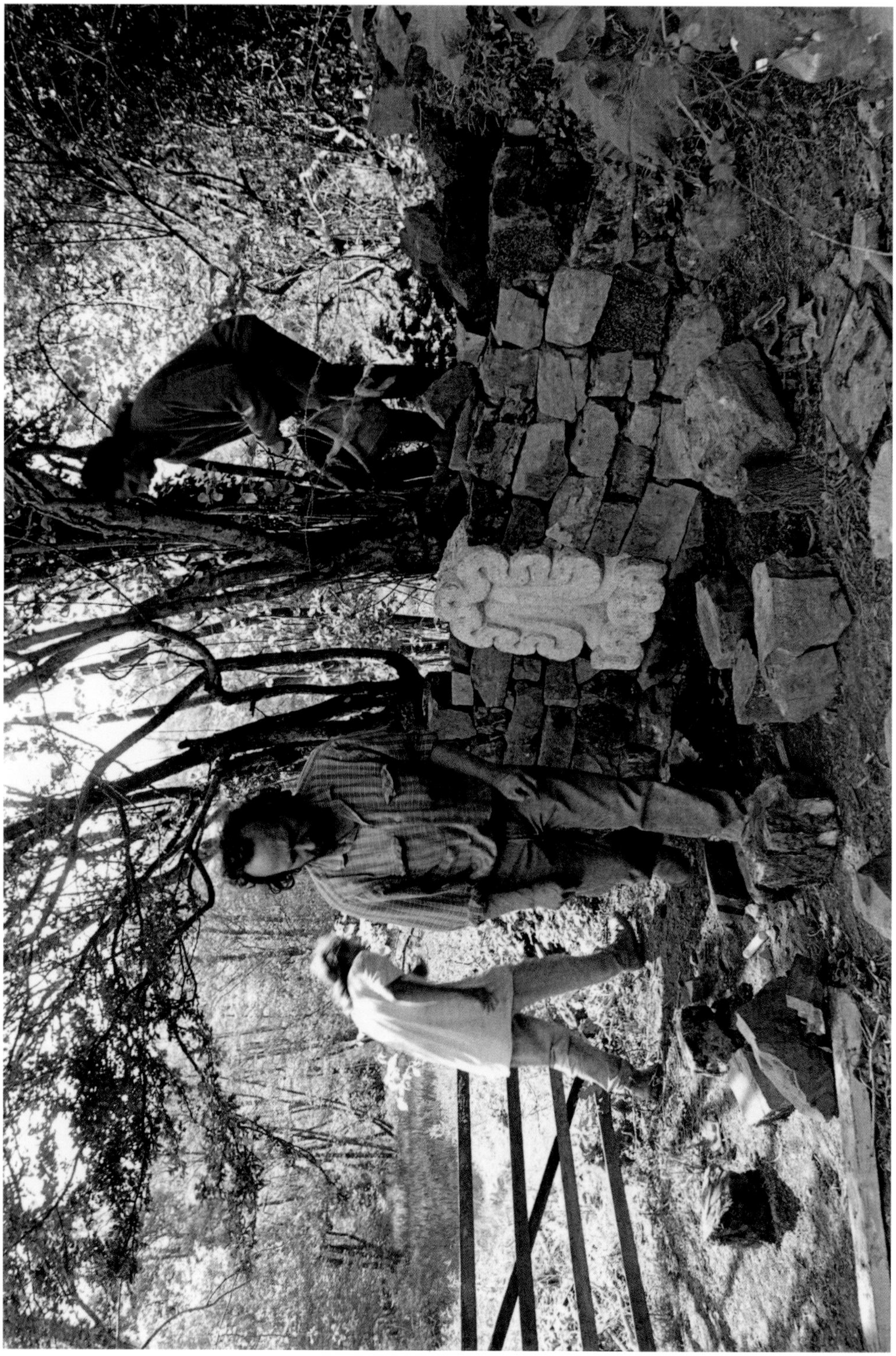

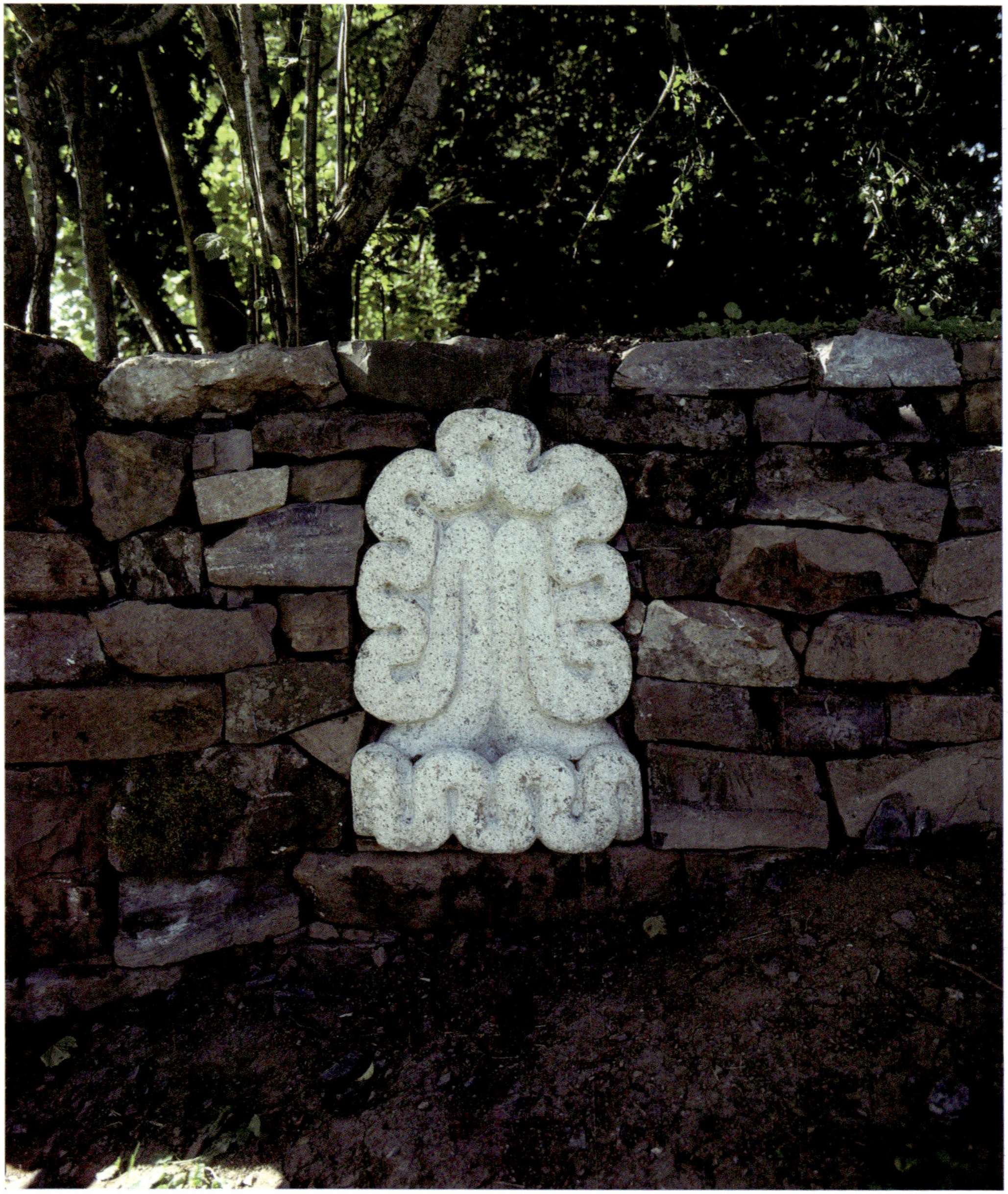

## QUOTATIONS

| | |
|---|---|
| PETER RANDALL-PAGE | Sculptor |
| CHRIS CHAPMAN | Photographer |
| TONY MILWARD | Clerk of the Parish Council |
| ELAINE CHUDLEY | Assistant at the Drewe Arms 1965-1995 |
| PENNY HILL | Proprietor of the Post Office |
| PHILIP MARKHAM | Dartmoor National Park Authority |
| HUGH MELLER | The National Trust |

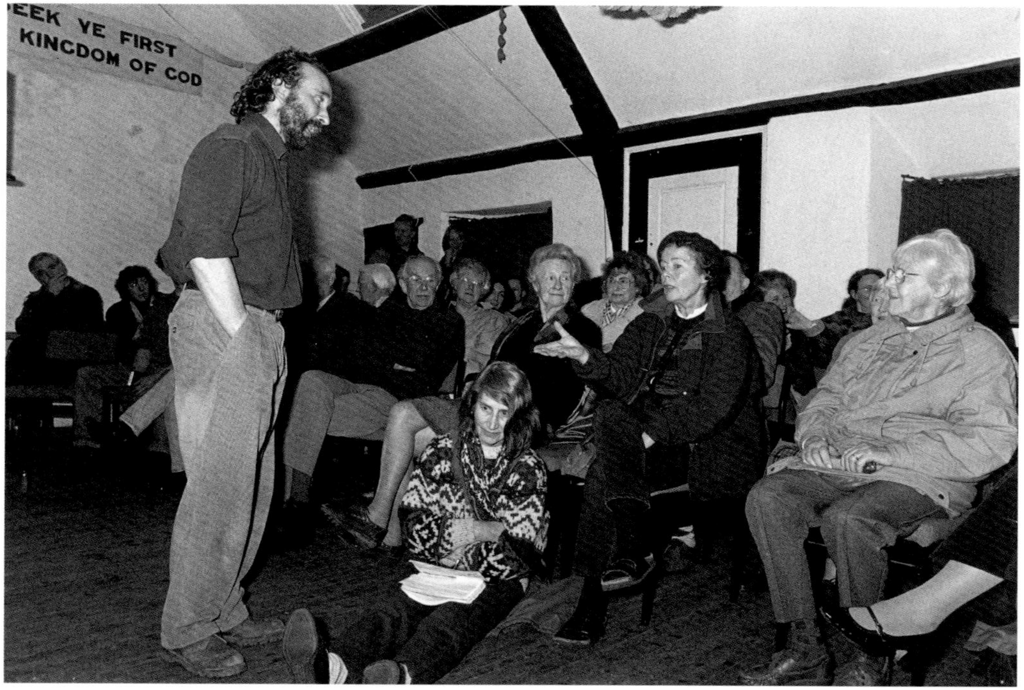

Photograph: Conrad de Courcy

PETER RANDALL-PAGE    Sculptor

Outside the Art Gallery, sculpture does not exist in isolation. The relationship of an object to a place and the people who inhabit that place is of utmost importance if the work is to have any real meaning. When Common Ground approached me with the idea of putting this concept into practice on public rights of way in the immediate locality of my home on the edge of Dartmoor, as part of the Local Distinctiveness campaign, it represented an exciting but daunting challenge. The area is one of exceptional natural beauty which is easily marred – and my audience are, for the most part, my friends and neighbours. I have tried to embed sculpture in the landscape, without the use of signs or labels. Discovering them by chance, I would like the experience to be direct, personal and unselfconscious. My hope is that the right object in the right place can set up a resonance, the effect of which may be more than the sum of its parts.

CHRIS CHAPMAN    Photographer

When I journey round my home environs, I am acutely aware of its layered history. Dartmoor's landscape has evolved, but at a very gentle pace, its granite heart yielding slowly to the efforts of man. These layers present themselves in many ways; the stone circles and megaliths of Bronze age, the scratchings and gouges of medieval tinners, the strong and solid buildings of church and farmhouse and the indelible character of its people and culture. The Local Distinctiveness project has added yet another dimension and my photographs are a celebration of this. I don't perceive Peter's wonderful sculptures as 'works' but rather as marks on the landscape, marks that have their roots in early man, but that are now speaking of the present. For me, they invoke a rising consciousness that is challenging and yet slow for us to learn; it is that Nature, man and his environment are, of course, all one and the same.

TONY MILWARD Clerk of the Parish Council

I was initially rather skeptical. After all, why should we who live in an area of considerable natural·beauty want to further enhance its distinctiveness? Then one day while walking on the Two Moors Way near Rushford Barton, I found this boulder apparently struck into two halves by a Levianthan geologist's hammer to reveal its intricately carved centre. Not a fossil, but a strangely compelling pattern, reminiscent of a giant walnut or a labyrinth – who knows. But certainly something that could have been there for a long time, in its rightful place, doing what was intended, focussing my eye on a particular part of the local landscape.

ELAINE CHUDLEY Assistant at the Drewe Arms 1965-1995

There was quite a lot of comment. In the pub everything was discussed, what these things were and what they were doing there. They don't scream at you, they tend to fit in with the local surroundings much more. You could almost go by without noticing sometimes. He's got the feel of the place and he loves it and it shows in his work, he doesn't want to alter anything he just wants to enhance things a little bit.

PENNY HILL Proprietor of the Post Office

Some people had this image that he was going to sculpt massive things and chuck them in the garden, they didn't understand that the garden was part of the sculpture or the sculpture was the garden and that the whole thing became a whole. It's just this balancing act and I think Peter found it by listening to everybody and taking everyone's views into account, he brought back a project with a little of everything in it. It's a home made effort, it's made in Drewsteignton. It means something because it's built by the community.

PHILIP MARKHAM    Dartmoor National Park Authority

My involvement with community schemes stretches back over a number of years and I know how difficult it is to achieve consensus for change. So often projects of this kind can be divisive, however good the design. I have therefore been impressed how hurt to these sensitivities has been minimised in drawing up the garden scheme, village views incorporated in the design and the emerging scheme thereby pulled the community together. The scheme reflects local materials and has truly grown from the local landscape with the involvement of the local people, introducing some new elements whilst retaining many of the old features dear to the local inhabitants.

HUGH MELLER    The National Trust

The sculpture in Whiddon Deer Park effortlessly complements its Dartmoor site both by the use of materials – granite and lead – and by its siting at the end of an ancient and ragged beech avenue astride the opening in a granite wall. It is made for the walker to chance upon and contemplate its sinuous patterns. These are reminiscent of the mazes on the floors of medieval cathedrals although here, instead of Chartres Cathedral soaring above, beech trees and distant views of Dartmoor are the accompaniment.

# VILLAGE GARDEN 1996

Granite and oak bench, granite bird-bath and table, granite and limestone paving, oak gate, dimensions of garden approximately 32m x 4.9m

Located in the village of Drewsteignton OS map ref. 735908

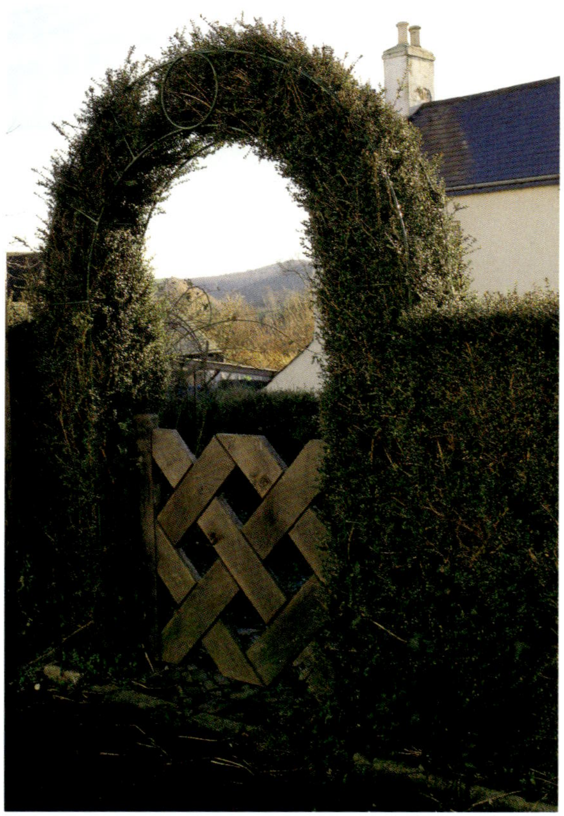

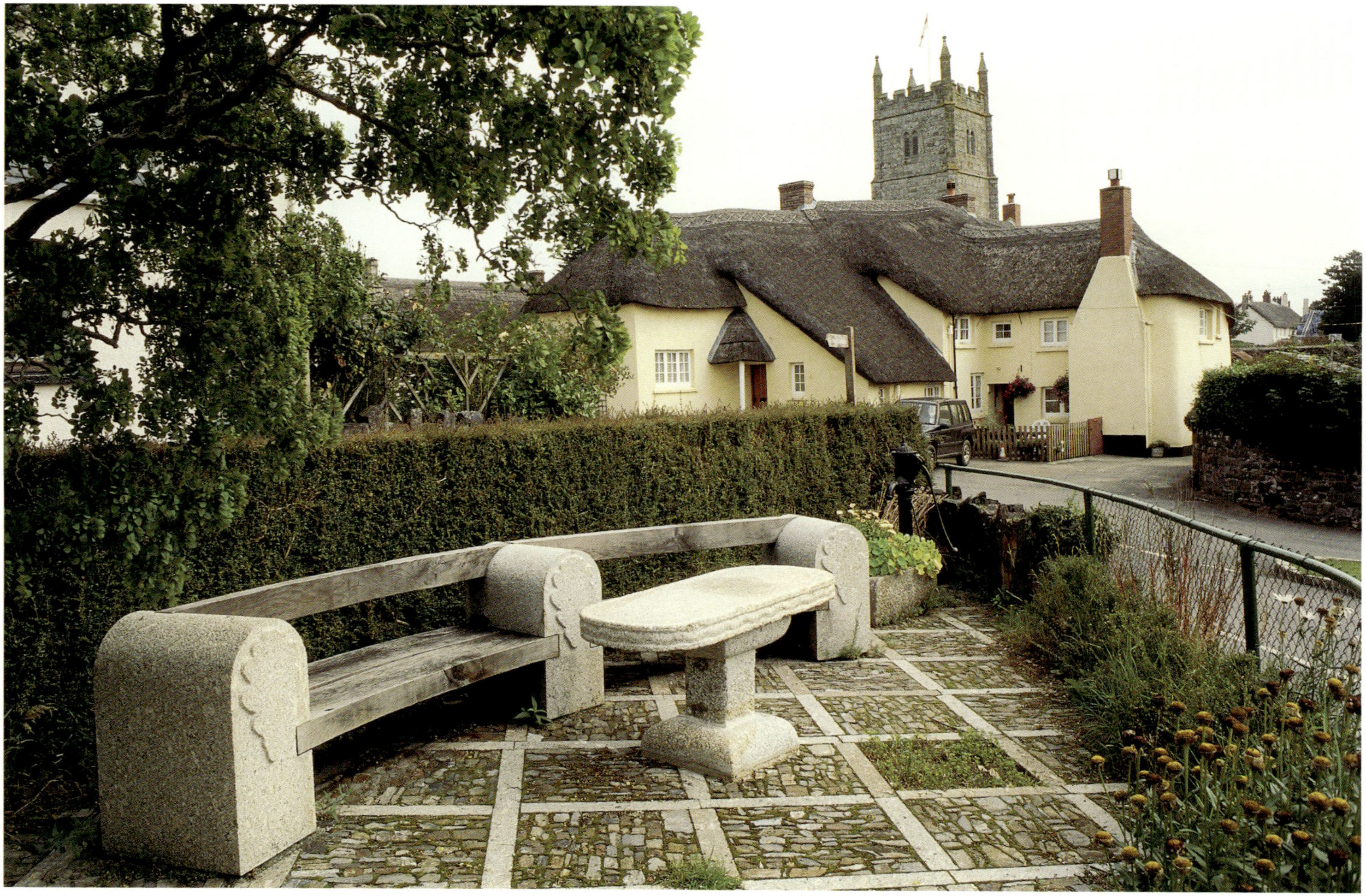

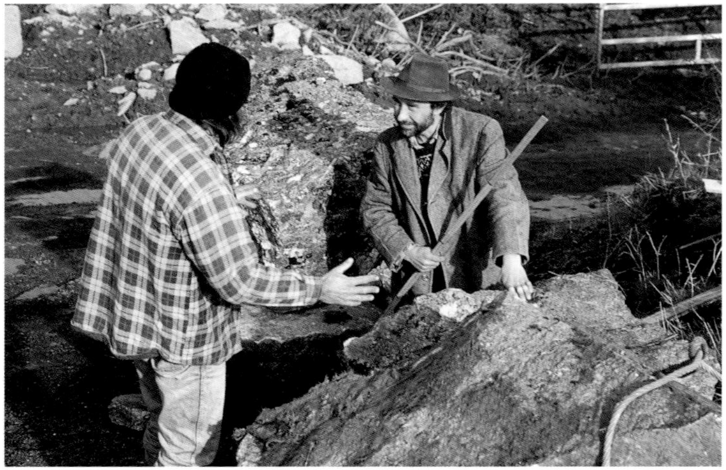
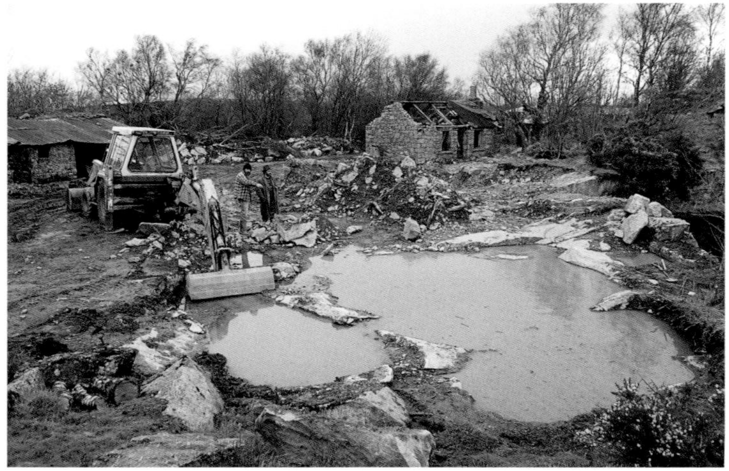
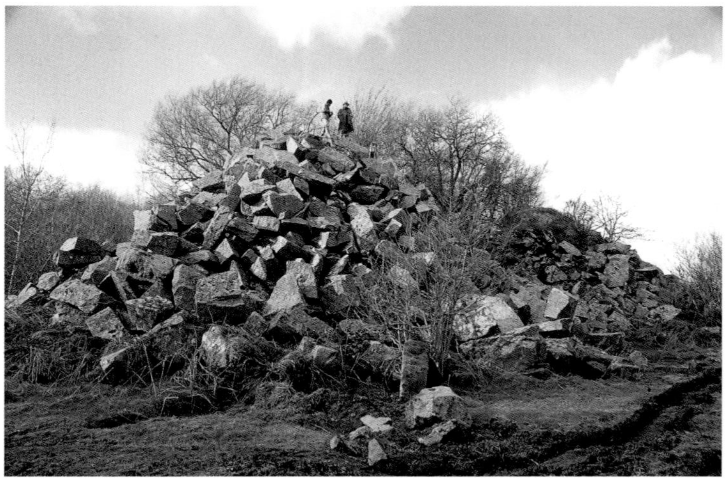
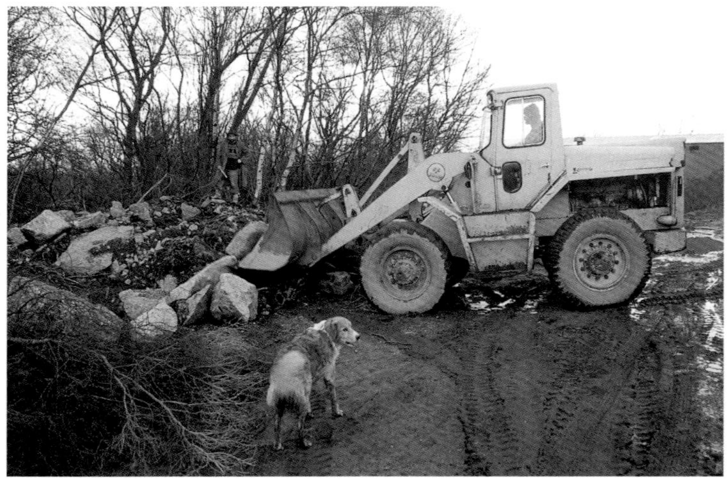

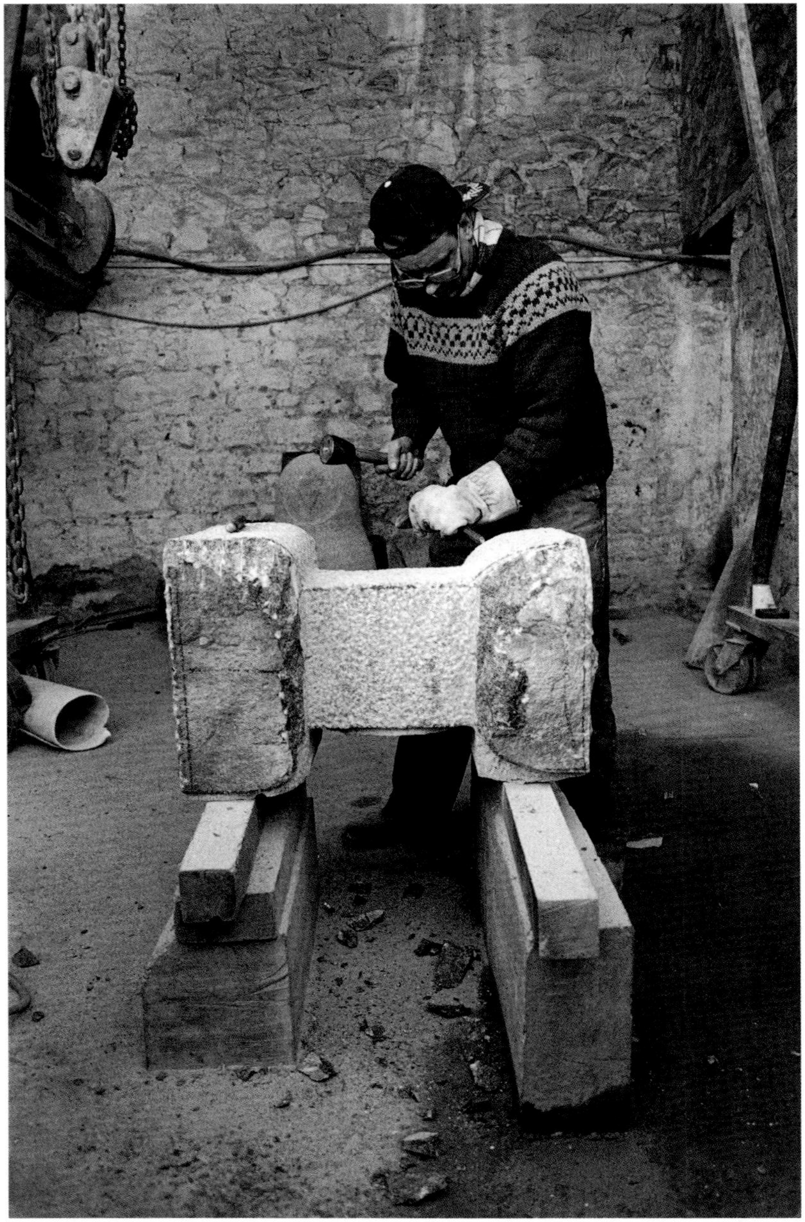

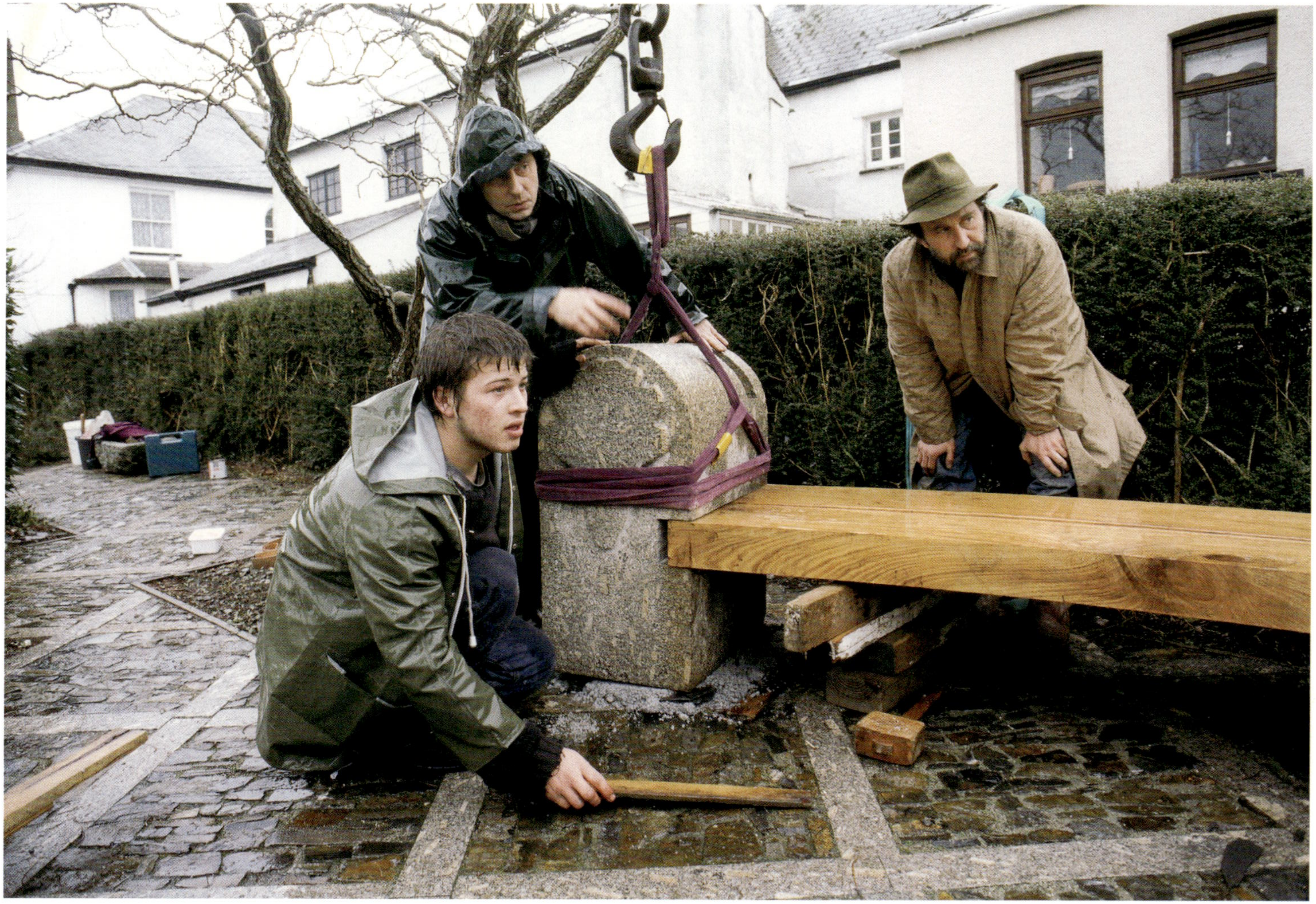

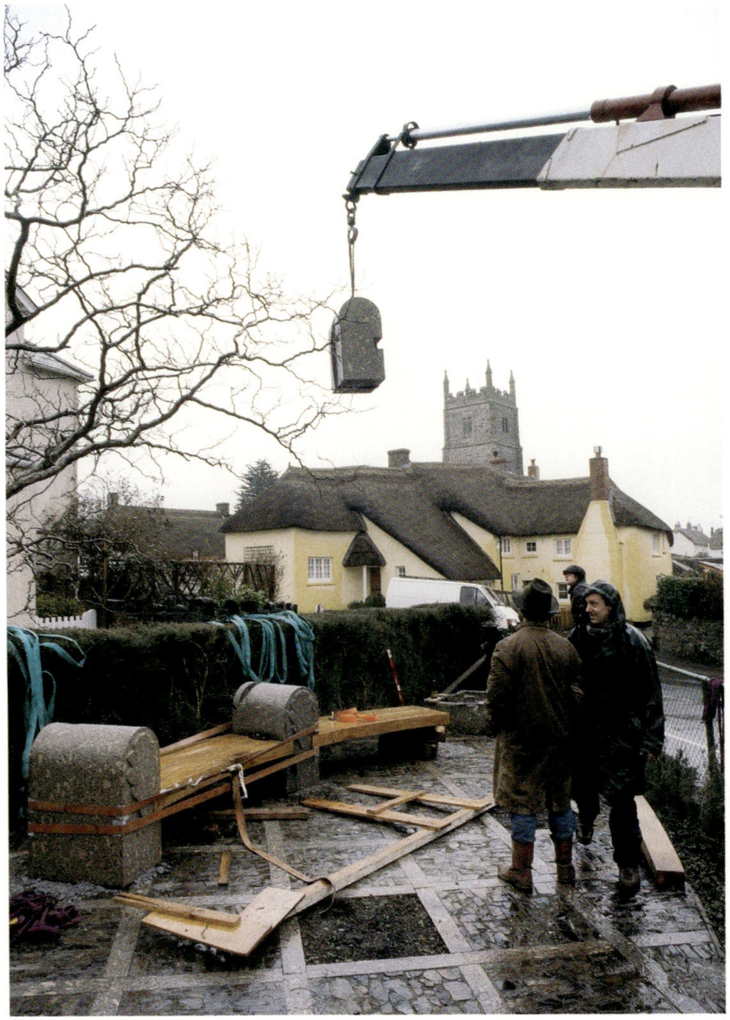

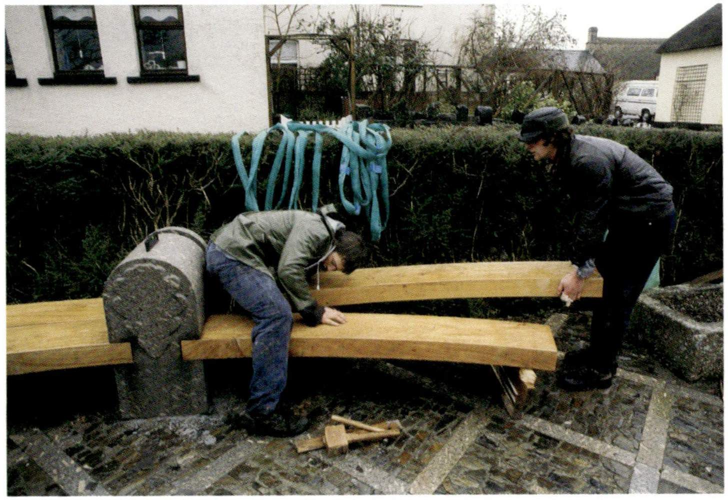

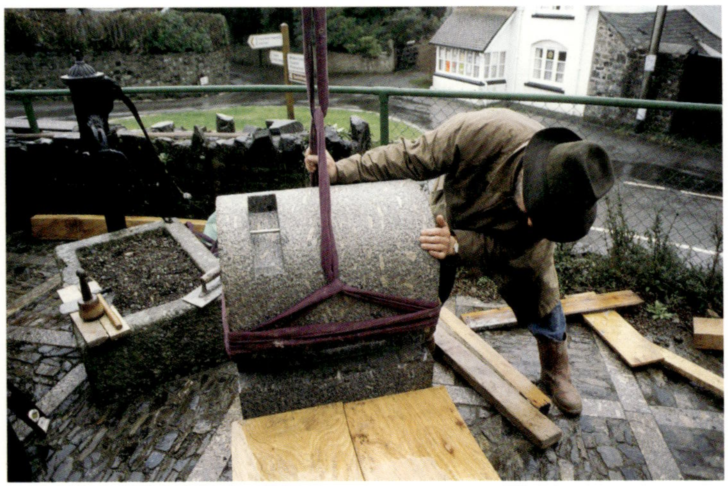

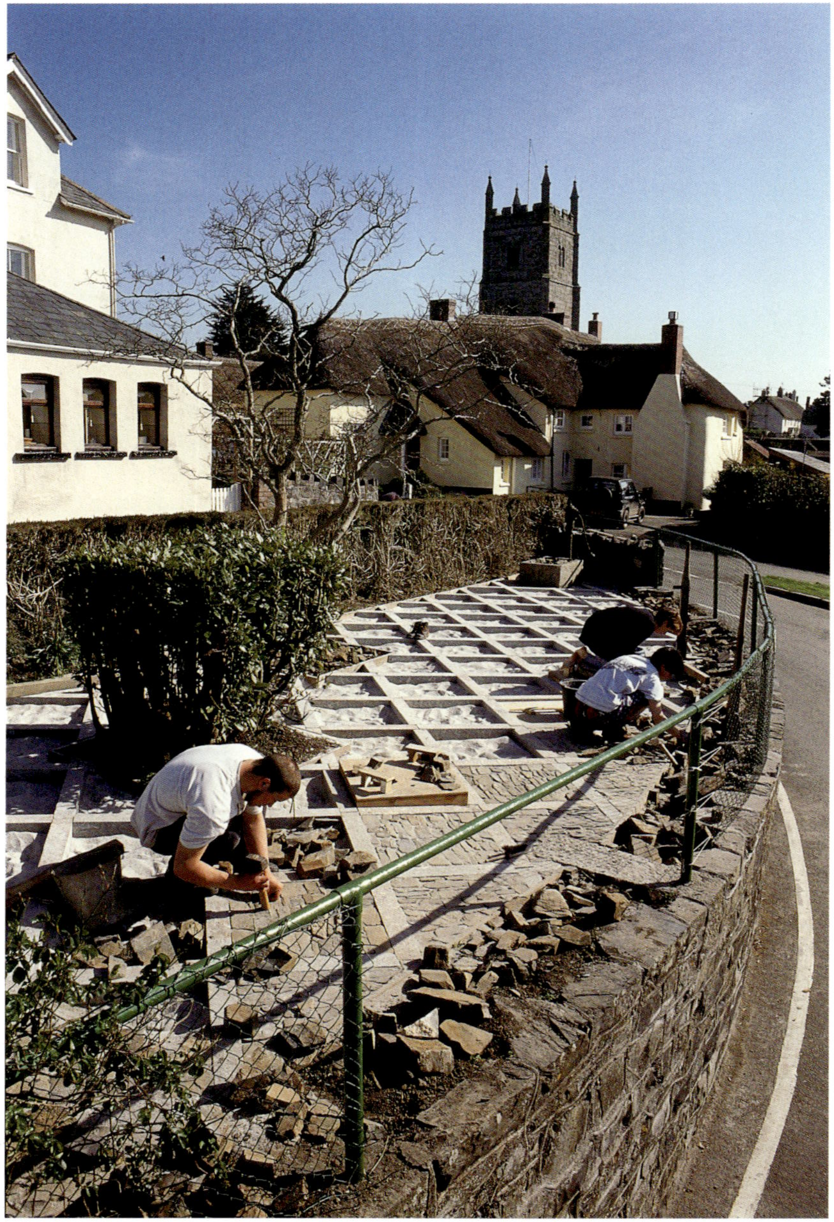

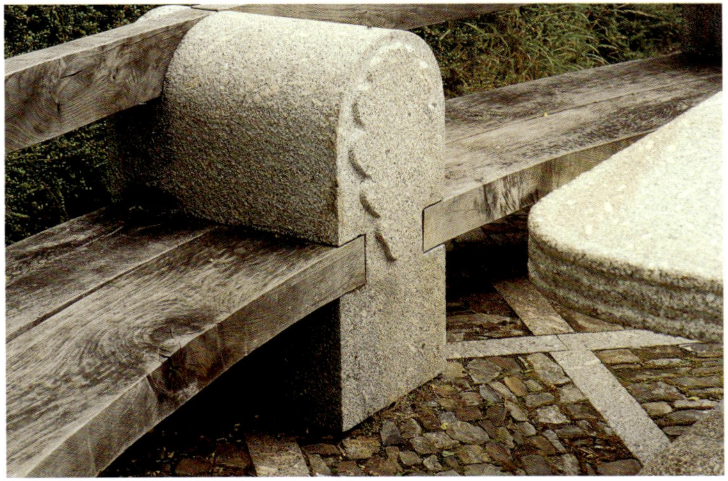
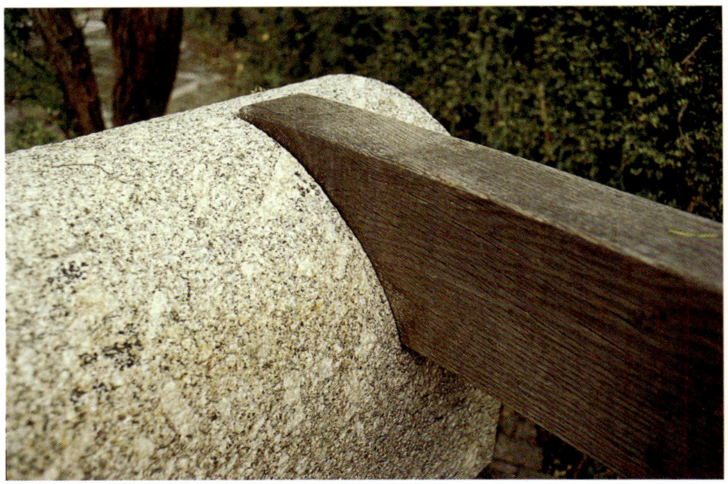
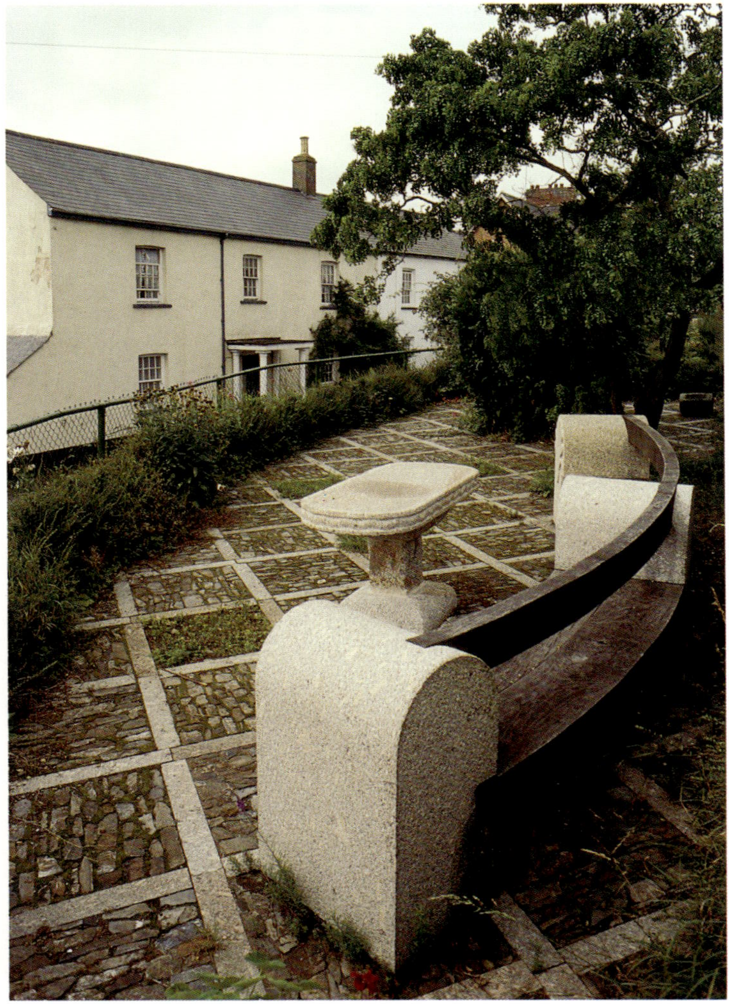

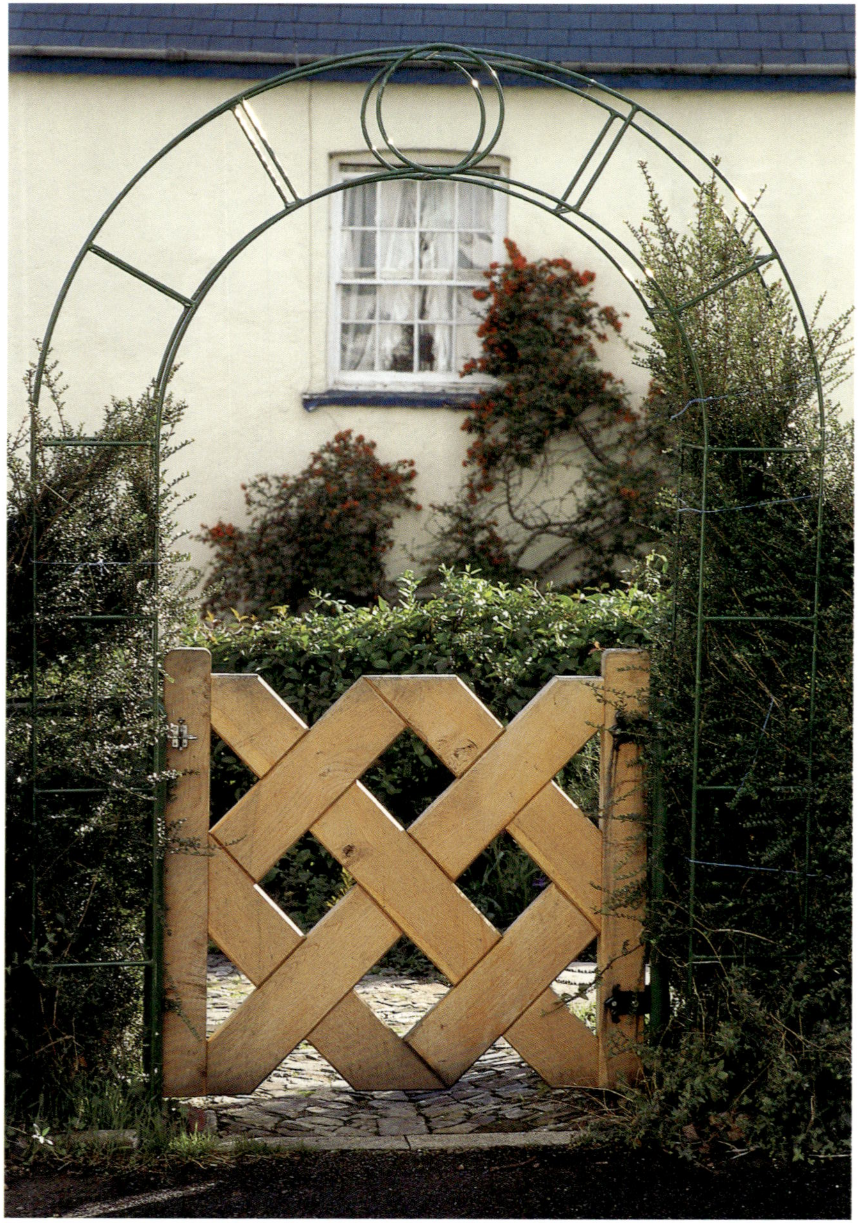

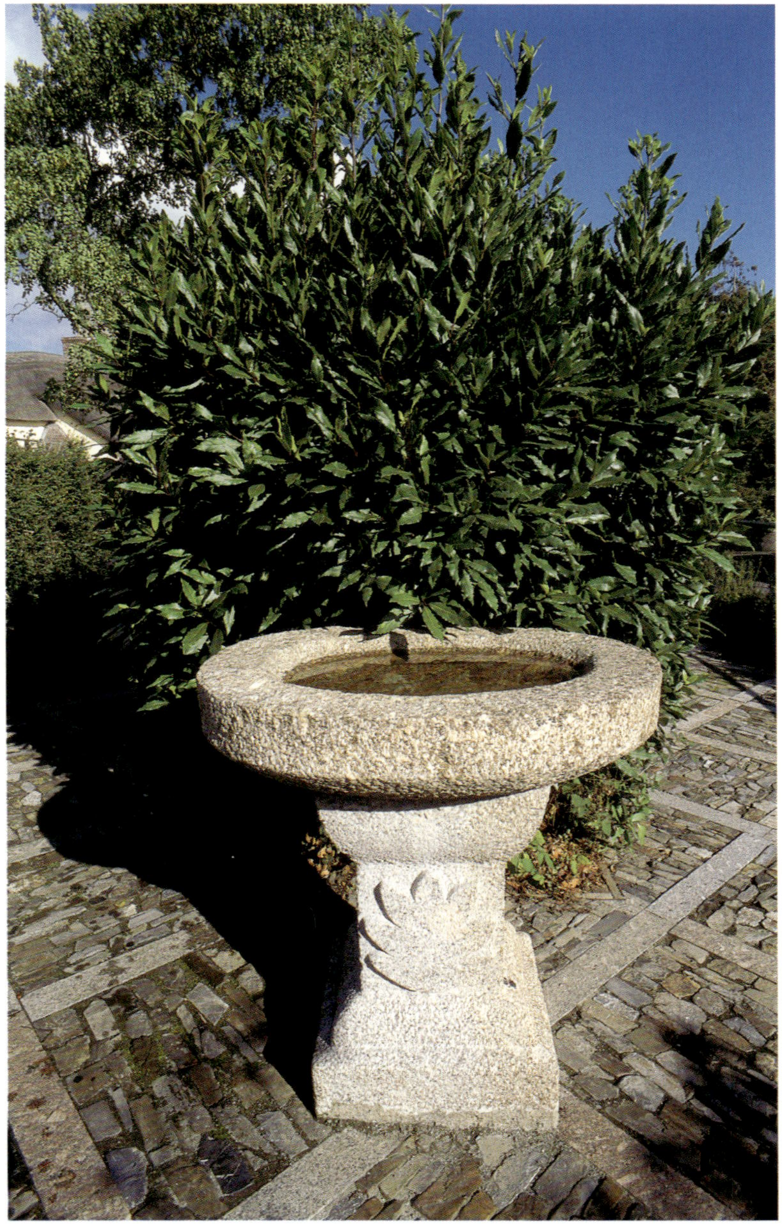

Many organisations and individuals helped make this project possible and special thanks go to:

Jacqueline Abey
Clive, Jill and Tom Adams
Garth Adams
Brian Beasley
Eric Blatchford
Marie Bond
David Brampton-Greene
Lise Bratton
Simon Butler
Elaine Chudley
Roger Chudley
Sue Clifford
Sarah Cox
Ben Craze
Matthew Diffey
PJ Dove
Pete Downey
Keith Gorman
Roger Harvey
Jane Hayter-Hames
Penny Hill
Dominic Hopkinson
Angela King
Mervyn Lillycrat
Philip Markham
Deborah Marsh
Mick McGlynn
Hugh Meller
Tony Milward
Jennifer Mullins
Pete Mullins
Graeme Murray
The late Rev. Charles Napier
Jean Partridge
Tim Peirce
Paul Petrie Richie
Colin Pink
The late Jack Price
Sara Roberts
Eric Robinson
Mike Rowe
Dougie Rowe
Jenny Scott
John Shiell
Simon Timms
Anthony Turner
Leo and Christine Van Leeuwen
Marina Warner
John Weir
Dominic Welch

Bardon Roadstone
Blackinstone Quarry
Common Ground
The Dartmoor National Park Authority
Devon Association of Local Councils
Devon County Council
Drewsteignton Parish Council
The Elephant Trust
The Elmgrant Trust
The Fleet Air Arm
Merrivale Quarry
The Henry Moore Foundation
The National Trust
Prudential Insurance plc
Rural Initiatives Fund
South West Arts

GRANITE SONG

Peter Randall-Page sculpture
Chris Chapman photography

A COMMON GROUND PROJECT

Published by Devon Books 1999
in association with Common Ground
with the support of
Prudential Insurance plc,
Devon County Council and
Dartmoor National Park Authority

Devon Books
Halsgrove House
Lower Moor Way
Tiverton
Devon EX16 6SS

Common Ground
PO Box 25309
London NW5 1ZA

Designed by Clive, Jill and Tom Adams

Printed by The Pale Green Press, London E3

ISBN 1 85522 685 5



Endpapers: details of Ordnance Survey maps, published 1906.

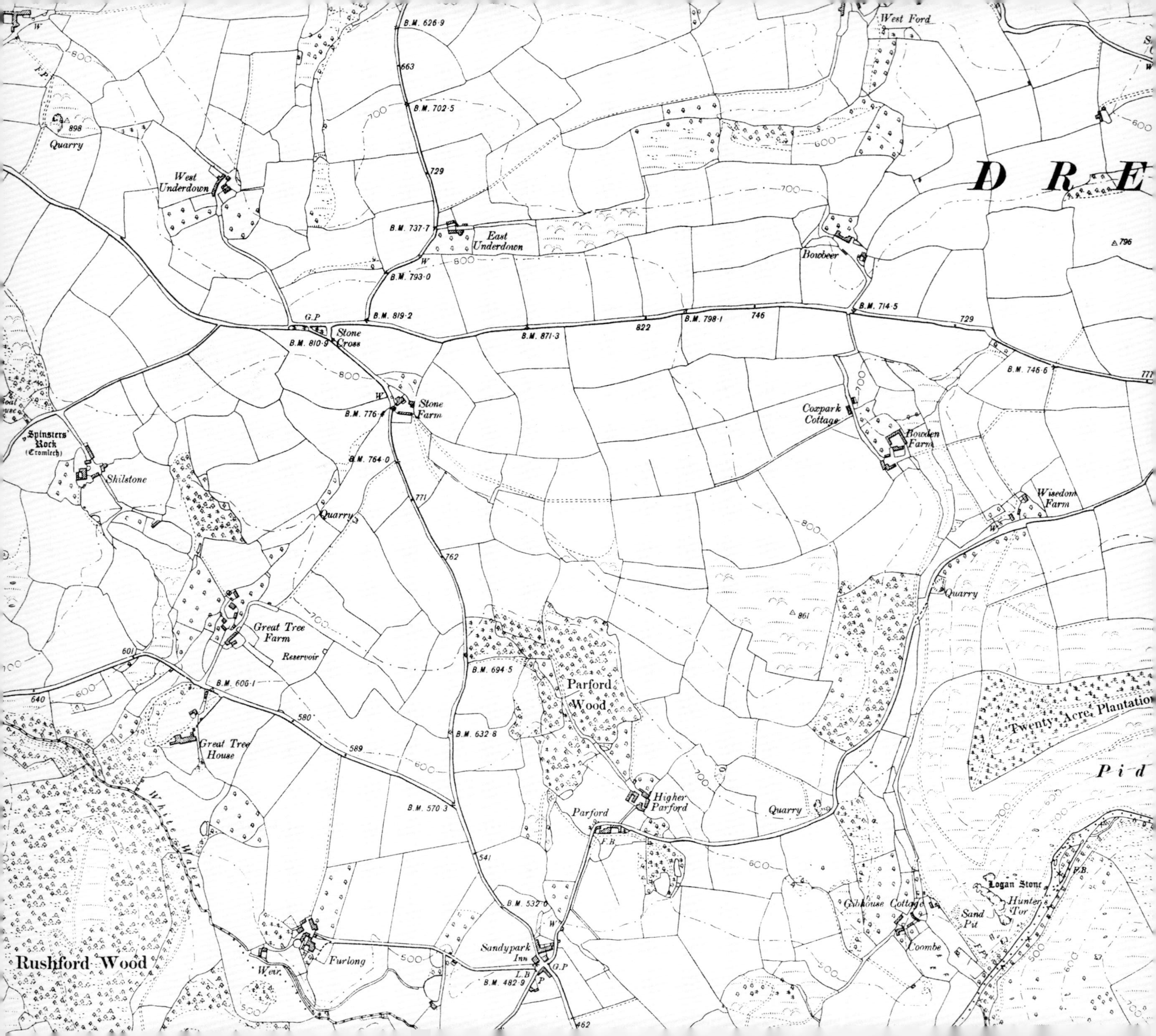

West Ford
Quarry
West Underdown
East Underdown
Bowbeer
D R E
Stone Cross
G.P
Stone Farm
Coxpark Cottage
Bowden Farm
Spinsters' Rock (Cromlech)
Shilstone
Wisedom Farm
Great Tree Farm
Reservoir
Parford Wood
Great Tree House
Twenty Acre Plantation
P i d
Higher Parford
Parford
White Water
Logan Stone
Hunter's Tor
Gibhouse Cottage
Sand Pit
Coombe
Sandypark Inn
Rushford Wood
Weir
Furlong